# A MAN'S GUIDE ON
# HOW TO SAVE YOUR
# MARRIAGE
# WITHOUT
# HAVING TO TALK ABOUT IT

## Doug Holt

# Dedication

This book is dedicated to YOU – The man who takes massive action. You are a remarkable individual who refuses to sit on the sidelines. Your commitment and drive inspire me, and our world needs more men like you.

While I couldn't have achieved this without the support of many people along my journey, I want to begin by expressing my deepest gratitude to my wife. She has been my rock, supporting me in my work and helping other men save their marriages, just as we saved ours. Her unwavering support enables me to continue my mission of assisting others. Without her, none of this would be possible. I love and appreciate her more than words can convey.

A heartfelt thank you also goes to my children, who often plead with me, saying, "Daddy, never go to work again!" Despite that, they walk me to my home office door every day, providing me with hugs and kisses to start my workday and showering me with love and excitement when I finish. They are my guiding lights, and I cherish them dearly.

I'd also like to express my gratitude to my partner in The Powerful Man movement and The Worldwide Movement nonprofit, Mr. Tim Matthews. You are not just a business partner; you are like a brother

to me. Your dedication and commitment to helping men tap into their true power is unparalleled. I consider myself blessed to have you by my side throughout this journey.

A special thank you goes to Darcy Curry, who has been my steadfast "work wife" for over a decade, allowing me to focus my efforts on helping others. You are a true superstar and that's why they call you Beyoncé!

I extend my appreciation to the coaches who took the time to read the rough draft and provide their valuable input, ensuring that this book would benefit thousands of men. Thank you, Andy Torr and Mark Smith. Alongside the other coaches at The Powerful Man, you work tirelessly to help guide men to the light in their darkest hour and beyond.

I would like to express my gratitude to Uday Rajaram, not only for reading through the rough draft but also for sharing how the book impacted him and his marriage. His comment served as a source of motivation when I felt weary at the keyboard, pushing me towards the finish line.

To my biological brothers, Brad Holt and Scott Holt, I want to say that I love both of you dearly. Even if we weren't related, I would choose you as my closest friends. Thank you for always lifting me up and leading by example.

I would like to extend my heartfelt gratitude to the incredible staff at The Powerful Man. Your unwavering dedication and commitment to our mission have been instrumental in transforming the lives of countless men. From the coaches who provide guidance and support, to the administrative team who ensures smooth operations, each of you plays a vital role in our success. Your passion, expertise, and tireless efforts truly make a difference in the lives of our clients, and I am deeply grateful for everything you do.

I would also like to express my deepest appreciation to the clients of The Powerful Man. It is an honor to be part of your journey of personal growth and transformation. Your trust in our programs and your willingness to embrace change inspire us every day. Witnessing your progress, witnessing the positive impact our work has on you and your families, is the most rewarding aspect of what we do. Your commitment to becoming the best versions of yourselves fuels our passion to continue serving and supporting you.

To the entire Powerful Man community, both the staff and the clients, thank you for your unwavering dedication to our shared mission. Together, we create a powerful network of support, encouragement, and growth. Your presence and participation are what make The Powerful Man truly remarkable. I am grateful to each and every one of you for being a part of this incredible journey.

# Table of Contents

# How It All Starts

When I got married, I was confident that our marriage was going to be one of the 50% with a fairy tale ending and not one of those sad cases that ended in divorce - I mean, what did those guys do wrong? They just didn't have what my wife and I had… boy was I wrong.

Did you know that every 13 seconds, there is one divorce in America? That equates to 277 divorces per hour, 6,646 divorces per day, 46,523 divorces per week, and 2,419,196 divorces per year. (https://gillespieshields.com/101-facts-about-divorce-in-2021/)

To top that off, nearly 70% of divorces are initiated by women. This is what an American Sociological Association (ASA) study from 2015 reports. Among college-educated women, this number jumps up to 90%.

I've been advising and coaching for over two decades. I don't say that to impress you but to impress upon you that even if I were a complete idiot, I'd still be able to pick up patterns. One of the patterns I've noticed is that when women start talking about leaving the marriage, they've been thinking about it for a long time and most likely have already formed their exit plan. It's us guys that wait and hope things will "work themselves out." I'm here to tell you it doesn't work that way, and the above statistics tell the story.

You, like me, are on a quest to be better. We don't accept things the way they are - especially when they aren't going the way we want them to. We're not going to accept being average. We aren't going to be another sad statistic.

I waited until my 30s to get married. I had a lot of fun being single. I was a business owner in Santa Barbara, California, and I didn't only own a gym but also a fitness magazine. Life was great…, but I distinctly remember looking out my office window one Saturday morning after a late night out, thinking, "I waited too long. All the good ones are taken, and I guess I'll be single forever." The type of woman I wanted, a woman I was willing to settle down with, was a fantasy.

That was until I met my wife.

My wife and I quickly connected, and both enjoyed similar things. She was fun, outgoing, and had a positive energy about her. It didn't hurt that she was a stunning personal trainer.

Things seemed to roll off her back, and she would laugh them away. Neither of us sweated the small stuff and would assume the other person's intentions were good.

Sure, we hit a few bumps in the road, but for the most part, we'd move past them fairly quickly, and when we were apart, we couldn't wait to see each other.

That is until things changed.

Shortly after we got married, things changed for the worse. There was a shift.

I was certain it was her.

The distance between us seemed to grow, and I couldn't understand why. Surely getting married would fix those little issues that had popped up when we were dating. Surely, the level of certainty and security would allow both of us to be freer, and the sex would be even more amazing, right?

Nope. That didn't happen.

Why could I go out in the world and conquer in business, sports, and other areas of my life, but when I came home, nothing I did seemed to work?

Our arguments progressed, and the days between intimacy became more frequent. Things began to become a little bit more uncomfortable. And as things became more uncomfortable between us, arguments started; something that we used to brush aside and laugh at became little bits of contentiousness and resentment over time.

I remember coming home, wanting so badly to go home as a king to my queen, and walking in the door wondering if I even belonged there. There were times when I would brush by my wife in the kitchen, and it felt more like an annoyance than a welcome touch. My wife had become like a roommate, a roommate with a ring.

We became roommates… and my wife wasn't the cool kind of roommate I had in college, where I'd come home and be greeted by a beer and an invitation to watch Sports Center.

No, my wife had become the kind of roommate that complained about everything I did… or didn't do… and how I did it.

She was a roommate with a ring… and an annoying one at that.

It was frustrating, to say the least, but I'm an entrepreneur, and I solve problems. I handle shit. So, I was determined to show her how good of a husband I was, and then she'd see how lucky she was to have me… then the respect and appreciation would flow with sex soon following.

She complained about the kitchen; fine, she would see the cleanest kitchen in the world.

She complained about the trash not getting taken out; fine, she would come home to empty trash bins.

I took half the day off work that day. I remember it clearly. It was a typical day in Santa Barbara, California, where we were living - the sun was out, the weather was that perfect 73 degrees, and although I wanted to be at the beach playing volleyball with my friends, I was determined to show my wife how lucky she was to have a man that would sacrifice his time to ensure she was happy. She was going to love me!

I put on a fresh pot of coffee, cranked up the music, and cleaned. I'm not talking about a surface clean that you do before someone comes over to visit, but a real clean - the get on your hands and knees and scrub under the couch type of clean. I was going to do the laundry, clean the kitchen, fluff the pillows… the whole nine yards.

When I was done, I was proud of myself. You know that feeling, chest puffed out as you survey your work.

My wife came home, and I was beaming from ear to ear. Surely she would drop to her knees in recognition of the king that stood before her. The man she married was not only providing financially but was also taking care of the house, so she didn't have to. Yup. I was the man, and she would see it once again.

As she entered the living room overlooking the kitchen, my wife set her things down, and I proudly explained what I had been doing all afternoon.

My wife looked at me with her big blue eyes and said…

"You didn't clean the grates on the stove."

I was devastated.

"I didn't clean the grates on the stove! I scrubbed the f'n toilets, cleaned the sink, did the dishes, did the laundry, and all you do is complain about the stove? This is ridiculous…." My tirade continued. I was triggered, and she was going to hear it.

After all, didn't she realize how lucky she was? Other women would die to have a husband like me - I thought to myself.

My wife turned and walked away. She was now hurt, I was angry, and the distance between us had just grown even more.

When I calmed down, I felt guilty that she was in our room crying. I felt ashamed that, as her husband, I just couldn't seem to get anything right. The guilt and the shame turned to anger, but not at her, rather anger at myself.

I was used to solving problems. I was used to finding the answers. I was used to being "the man," but at home, I just couldn't get it right.

I tried audiobooks, couples therapy, and even podcasts, but the advice was always the same: just deal with it, take your wife on a trip, or keep talking about the problems from the past.

None of it worked, and most of the advice just seemed to make things worse.

This went on for some time, and my wife and I continued to try counselor after counselor - often walking out of the session more angry and upset than when we went in.

You see, marriage counselors are focused on the past and the problem, putting your entire focus on the things that are going bad. Granted, 90% of the things in our marriage were going right, and only 10% were going wrong, but if you spend your time together focusing on that 10%, that 10% becomes your focal point and pushes you further apart.

I recall one marriage counseling session where my wife and I sat on that awkward couch that so many of us men find ourselves on, looking at the counselor sitting before us. We were "okay" but clearly not sitting close to each other.

As the session progressed, it felt as if my wife and I were competing to get the counselor on our side. If only they could see my side of things, I thought, then this could be over quickly. She was clearly to blame. Sure, I had my issues, but they were minor - like working a bit longer than normal, but that was so we could afford to live the life she wanted to live, I would tell myself.

We were focusing on the past, where everything was terrible, and we realized we weren't going in the direction we wanted to. It's like getting into a high-performance sports car; you want to go forward. You want to go fast because you're in a sports car; you're in a high-performance vehicle. You're always looking in the rearview mirror. While stepping on the gas and trying to accelerate, you're bound to hit trees, curbs, and pedestrians along the way, leaving total carnage.

That's what marital counseling was like for us - driving fast but looking backward while trying to move forward.

Every time we walked out, there was more carnage on the road of our love and our relationship. I remember my wife looking at me one day crying, saying, "we both love each other...why is this so hard?" And me, the man with all the answers, the leader, not knowing and not being able to say anything, just wanting to get up and walk away and have the pain end. For this all to be over.

By the end of the counseling session, we were more pissed off than when we went in. I could feel her anger, and she could feel mine. It was palpable.

As we exited the therapy room and came to the waiting area, there sat another business owner with his wife, whom we knew well.

He and I caught each other's eyes, and after a split second of shock, we both started laughing.

I walked by them, said, "Good luck!" and walked out the door.

My wife and I had dinner reservations at one of the nicest restaurants in town. We proceed to dinner, not saying a word to each other. We were that couple you see at the restaurant who you can tell want nothing to do with each other. What's worse is that at this time, I owned several businesses in the town, so I not only knew the owners of the restaurant well, but I also knew many of the patrons. The mask was on, but we were both so upset at each other that we no longer cared who noticed or what they thought.

The power couple in the public eye had been exposed.

We weren't perfect, and this wasn't working.

Then I decided to leave.

Little did I know...my wife was on the same carousel, investigating her options on how to exit our marriage and thinking it was me that needed fixing, not her.

I knew that I was entitled to more. I mean, after all, I worked my ass off! I brought home money, helped out around the house, and did everything she was asking me to do at the time. Everybody else thought it was great. Why didn't she? Obviously, there was something wrong with her! It was her that needed fixing.

I needed a break, so I left home for three weeks and stayed at a beautiful condo on the beach in San Diego, California.

While in San Diego, I was determined to figure out what went wrong and how I could exit this horrible marriage.

Clearly, she wasn't working on the problems she needed to work on, and I was tired of feeling disrespected and not honored for the man I was. I knew that I could go out and get a woman who would love, respect, and take care of me, all the things I thought my wife would do. Yet, she didn't seem to want to step up and fix the things she needed to fix.

I remember thinking, "if only she would change,"

I mean, really, what was my wife thinking?

Didn't she know how amazing I was?

During my time there on the beach by myself, I started to reflect.

That's when it hit me.

I remember distinctly running on the beach one morning with the waves crashing and the salty air hitting my face, and I asked myself a question. Was I being the absolute best husband I could possibly be? Of course, the answer came back "no." I grimaced a bit but continued.

Then I asked myself, "Am I being the best version of myself I can be?" Again, as the waves hit my face as I was going in stride, the answer came back. "no." This wasn't making me feel good, but I knew it was the truth.

I then asked myself a third and final question. "If I leave this marriage and go on to date or be with somebody else, am I bringing the best version of myself into this new relationship? The answer again was "no."

That's when I realized that if I took the time to work on myself instead of focusing on my wife's shortcomings, my stock would go up.

You see, at that moment, I saw myself, just like I saw any stock you would buy in the stock market. If you chose to buy Apple stock, you would only purchase the stock if you thought that stock would increase in value. I started to wonder if my stock, in relation to the way I was showing up in my marriage from my wife's perception, had been increasing or decreasing in value.

Was I showing up as the best man I could be? Was I "stepping to the line," as we say at The Powerful Man? Or was I backing down when times got tough, not showing up fully in my marriage or life?

That was a hard pill to swallow.

I decided it was time for me to double down on increasing my stock value, whether it be a sexual market value or just value in general. At that moment, it became clear that by increasing my value, my wife would see how amazing I was and make all the changes in her life. Or

I would leave, and in leaving the marriage, I would come out a better and more valuable man in the eyes of the marketplace.

I would then meet even more amazing women who I could currently attract into my sphere of influence now.

I decided that there was one thing that I could control. And guess what? It wasn't my wife. The one thing that I could control was me.

The actions I took, the thoughts I thought, and the feelings I chose to feel were all that I could control; it's with the idea of extreme ownership that spurred me to move forward.

The worst-case scenario was that I left this relationship, and now I would leave a better man; there was no real downside to the situation. In the best-case scenario, I become a better man, my wife recognizes my greatness, and then she'll make changes within herself.

As I like to call it, The Pivot, was really when I went from victimhood, blaming my wife and the external things outside of me, to taking full ownership of all that I could control.

That's when I set out on a quest; a quest to learn why my wife and I had had these problems. A quest to find out not only the problems but also what solutions could come about.

I also knew that once I could improve upon myself, nobody would have control over me. Only myself. How could I expect anyone else to live up to their full potential if I wasn't living up to mine? That's when I found myself signing up in San Diego for a boxing gym, going to work out, waking up early to do a morning routine, and reading and focusing on my personal goals.

This time, my goals didn't include my wife. My goal list included things I wanted to do, things I wanted to accomplish, and things I wanted to do for myself, but not necessarily by myself.

I started to think of this new path, this new way of thinking and understanding my situation, as if I were going on a long road trip. There was no doubt in my mind that I was going. I was steadfast. I would invite my wife to come along for the ride. The seat next to me, the co-pilot seat, was reserved for her (for now), but if she didn't want to join me, I was at peace with her choice because I was going no matter what. Not for her. I was going for me. I wanted her next to me, and I would be clear with her about that, but I would also be clear that I was going with her or without her.

And hey, if she chose not to join me, you never know who I might meet along the way who would love to tag along for the ride. It was that feeling of determination and clarity that set me forward on my path.

I gave myself 30 days, and I dedicated myself to this endeavor, just as I had dedicated myself to learning how to program a computer, learning to run a business, or tackle a new skill. I went all in. I stepped to the line.

The result?

I was able to turn my marriage around from one of complete disaster, where both of us were talking to divorce attorneys, to one where my wife looks at me with love, respect, and admiration. From a marriage where every day felt like a struggle to one where we both look forward to seeing each other. Instead of viewing each other as enemies, we now support each other as a team.

And you know what? I did this all without having to ask, or tell, my wife to do anything. She followed my lead, and that's what this book will teach you to do.

I've spent almost ten years working on creating a system to help other men, just like you, go from a sexless, failing marriage to one where your wife looks at you again with love and respect… even if you're on the brink of divorce.

Along with Tim Matthews and the other coaches at The Powerful Man, we've used this methodology to help thousands of men do the same.

This methodology has been fine-tuned and turned into something that we call The Activation Method at The Powerful Man.

I'm going to share with you the same tenets that we have shared with thousands of other men who have successfully turned their marriages from the brink of divorce into a relationship they couldn't have even imagined was possible. I wrote this book so you could read it chapter by chapter or jump to specific chapters for reference.

As always, we're continuously changing the program as we find things that will better help and serve the men. I will do my best to update this book and put updates on the Powerful Man website so you can get the latest information. Visit www.ThePowerfulMan.com/book to check for regular updates.

If you have any hesitations about whether you have the power to change your marriage, I encourage you to look at the stories of other men who, like you, were in the pit of despair before turning things around.

I truly believe that men, as leaders of their households, can not only save their marriages but also lead their communities to create a better world. That is the reason I started this book. This is the book I wish I had had when my wife and I were going through our dark period. It didn't exist. And I had to go through years of trial and tribulation to figure this out myself.

Since discovering my path, I've worked with great coaches through The Powerful Man, an international movement of business owners and men coaching 1000s of men to achieve the same results that I did—the same results you're hoping for in this book. My sincere wish for you is that if you put in the work and do the exercises that I'm going to present, you will see massive shifts in your marriage.

I'm not going to tell you that this book is guaranteed to work for you. Some men leave it too late, or there are extenuating circumstances that are too far gone, such as physical abuse or their partner having mental health issues. This does happen. Some marriages are just too far gone. You see, most men like me, and maybe you, wait way too late to work on their marriages. We wait until the house is on fire before we take action. As men, we wait until our wife is one, or maybe two, feet out the door before we put in any effort...before we grab a book like this.

Or maybe you're like me, and you started listening to podcasts and grabbing audiobooks or other books that weren't effective. They were written by people who had a lot of theory but not a lot of in-the-trenches experience. Not the "in the trenches" experience of working with men like us - leaders, business owners, and men striving to not only save their marriages but better themselves and their families, as well as their communities.

As a man, a husband, a father, and a leader, they utilize that to raise their stock. You see, when my wife married me, she was betting on me. She made a bet. Not only was I the right guy for that time, but I would be the right guy for the next 10, 20, 30, and 40 years, and my stock would go up. I do the same thing when investing in stocks, real estate, or anything else. I'm investing my capital and money in the hopes that whatever I'm investing in will increase in value. Your wife and my wife are doing the same thing with us.

Now, it's not too late.

What you're going to do here is increase your value. Your wife is going to see that as well, and it's going to pull her back in if it is too late for you, and I hope it isn't.

Not all men take action fast enough, and if the marriage is too far gone, then the silver lining here is that you're going to come out the other side of doing this work as a man who's worth more in the sexual marketplace. You'll also find an inner peace that you haven't known for a very long time, if ever. I've seen this happen countless times with men.

So, again, how did you end up with this book in your hands?

As I said, you, like me, are striving for something better, better in your relationship, and better, in particular, in your marriage. Maybe you've seen me on shows, attended a seminar that I was a part of, or maybe, just maybe, you've been passed this book by another man, a powerful man who's walked this path and journey before. And you could tell something was different about that man; he had that thing about him that attracted everybody to him.

At The Powerful Man, that thing is known as being "Activated." I'll go into this later, but this man gave you a book because he saw something in you.

He saw in you the man he used to be and knew the man who could come out the other side.

How did I come to write this book? Well, I've dedicated my professional career to helping men like you overcome obstacles that I have faced and tens of thousands of other men just like you have faced and overcome. This isn't just theory. Yes, I've taken the classes and read the books, but more importantly, I've applied these concepts to my personal life and the lives of thousands of men, just like you, with proven results time after time.

This is where theory meets in-the-trenches, real-world practice. And that, my friend, equals results. Look, you've already bought the book. I'm not selling you anything here. I'm just telling you that if you commit yourself to doing the work as it is laid out here, you will see excellent results.

Now I say that to you because I know me, the old me; let's call him Doug 1.0. The old me tended to start books, stop them, or maybe read a book or listen to an audiobook but not fully participate in the exercises. I would often say to myself, "Yeah, yeah, I already know that." Or "yeah, I'll do that later." I'm begging you, encouraging you, and imploring you not to be like the old me.

I'm simply a man who has been down the road you are currently on, coming back to tell you, "Hey, the road you've been on... the bridge is broken. You can't get past it; you're just going to crash. You can see the smoke in the air from all the other wrecks. But there's another road, a path that's smoother and shorter. It's also much more scenic and enjoyable, and I want you to enjoy this journey the best you can because it is beautiful, and you deserve that."

Don't go down the broken path.

Commit now, here at this moment as you read these words on these pages, to dedicate yourself to whatever time you need each day to master the principles in this book: 30 minutes to an hour a day. You know your relationship is worth it, right?

I encourage you to join our free online community of men like you. It's been said that you become the product of the five people you spend the most time with, so why not surround yourself with men who are here to better themselves, for themselves, their families, and their communities? Simply go over to www.ThePowerfulMan.com/book to get access. It's free, so there really isn't any reason not to dive right in.

Now let's get started.

As always, I'm in your corner.

# The Pivot

Somewhere along the lines, as your relationship was moving along, something shifted. You see, when you first got married or started dating, it seemed like you couldn't go wrong.

A fart on the couch became a joke, and both of you would giggle.

Think back to when you and your wife were first together. There were magical times that seemed to last forever. There was a time when your wife could melt your heart when she looked at you with those loving and trusting eyes. Those were the good old days.

Now, if you pass gas, it's a major offense.

Think of the health of your relationship like the scales of justice, where you have "Good Feelings and Experiences" on one side of the scale and "Bad Feelings and Experiences" on the other side.

When you start off in your relationship, the scale is heavily weighted with good experiences and emotions. So much so that you could almost get away with murder and still be loved by your wife or then-girlfriend.

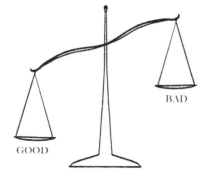

As you learn about each other or go on dates, you would add to the "good" side of the scale. It took some effort to plan dates, but otherwise, it most likely felt easy. You were drawn to her, and she was drawn to you—like two magnets sticking together.

You would go to the ends of the earth for each other.

You were laughing hysterically together, and she thought your jokes were actually funny. She was looking into your eyes with love, respect, and admiration. You were her everything.

Somewhere along this journey, things started to slip. Chances are, it wasn't noticeable at first. Perhaps you tossed some kids into the mix, thus making sleep and personal time a thing of the past. Maybe for you, work got tougher, and you spent more time at the office trying to provide for your family. Or maybe a once-in-a-lifetime pandemic changed everything for your family and forced you all to stay in the same house while fear and uncertainty set in. Whatever it was, you and your wife started to drift apart.

And during this time, little things started to add up to the point where the scale began to tip out of your favor. The bad experiences slowly outweighed the good ones, and distance became greater.

You went to bed one night, realizing that you and your wife were six inches apart, yet it felt like you were miles away from one another. Many men quickly give up on the idea of reaching out to hug their wives because they know they will be turned down. So, we roll over, hoping that tomorrow

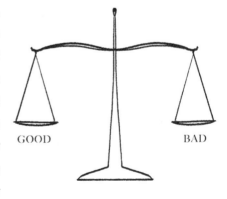

GOOD                    BAD

will be a better day, yet you can feel the distance and the loneliness as you lay there.

The anxiety and sadness that come during those sleepless nights can be crippling and creep into the next day as you head off to work, wondering if this will ever change.

Over time, you started to notice the scales had not only shifted, but they weren't even level. The scales had tipped so far out of order that the bad experiences and emotions outweighed the good ones. This led to arguments over seemingly little things: the slightest indiscretion or even a movement in the wrong direction would ignite a fight.

I can recall when this happened to me, coming home one day from work after absolutely crushing the day, only to find myself reaching for the doorknob and not wanting to go in. I wasn't sure what I was going to get when I walked through that door, but I was pretty certain that it wasn't going to be fun. Perhaps I wouldn't get criticized, and she would just ignore me instead. Perhaps she would also be in a good mood, and maybe, just maybe, we could have some fun. Doubtful, but it could happen...

Sex, or at least good, connected sex, is uncommon for most men at this point. Some men turn to porn, while others turn to affairs, not knowing that their wives are doing the same.

She starts spending more time on her phone, texting, or on social media. When you walk in the room, perhaps she gets a little annoyed or even secretive about what she's doing.

A love song comes on the radio, and your wife might start singing it, but you know she's no longer thinking about you. She may even start going out with her friends at night more often, leaving you at home to tend to the kids and the house.

What most men don't realize is that women are far more likely to have an affair, emotional or physical, than their husbands. The media plays it up as if we're the ones out late at night being unfaithful, but in my experience, it's far more often the wives that actually take action and stray. The truth is that women are just better at covering it up, and they have a lot more opportunities than their husbands to find someone else to be with. It happens more than you might think.

When the scales are tipped so badly in the wrong direction, it seems like you can do nothing right, and the relationship is over. Dead. Or is it?

In this book, I'm going to talk about what happened to cause the scales to tip out of your favor so that you can make sure that that never happens again. And, of course, I'm not only going to help you bring the scales back to neutral, which will feel like an amazing place to be since it's been so long since you've been able to even be at that level. But I will show you how to tip the scales back in your favor so that the good feelings and experiences far outweigh the bad ones, and how to keep them there forever.

# The 5 Agonies of No Man's Land

What happens for many men is that they enter a place that we call "No Man's Land"—a place where they're absolutely lost.

They've lost connection with their partner, connection with themselves, and connection with their dreams. They know there's more to life, but they feel stuck and unsure how to get out. No Man's Land can make a man feel rejected, low, and angry at the world because this isn't how it's supposed to work out. This isn't the life he was meant to live.

You've been sold a dream: if you work hard, put your head down, and be a good guy, then everyone will love you.

But that didn't happen, did it?

You work hard to provide for your family, but now you feel like you're just a paycheck. Your wife and kids look at you with contempt, except when they need something.

Many men I speak to feel that their families would be better off without them, and they use a permanent solution, suicide, to solve a temporary problem. This isn't the solution, and if this is running through your head, I encourage you to reach out to a professional immediately.

Suicide is the second leading cause of death among men 13 to 44 years of age. Unintentional Injuries is number one, and I believe that many of those deaths are men covering up their suicide so their families can get the insurance money. Yes, even in death, we men try to provide for our families.

After working with many men on this path, I can tell you that it does get better; hold on and reach out for help. I've provided some resources for you here: www.ThePoweruflMan.com/book.

In this place of No Man's Land, a man will face five agonies.

The first agony is the agony of greed.

The agony of greed doesn't just have to do with money. The agony of greed is where there's always a feeling of perpetual emptiness, as if no amount of money, success, or material possessions could ever fill the void within a man. The agony of greed leaves the man feeling hollow and empty.

Often, men will try to fill this void by buying a nice car, a watch, or perhaps a second home on the lake, all hoping to have that "thing" that will make them feel happy. Often, it does, but only for a very short time. So they buy the next thing or go on the next adventure, but they can still feel the void in the pit of their stomach, so they push themselves to do more... to have more. In the end, the feeling of emptiness doesn't go away, it expands.

And this agony of greed leads to the second agony, which is the agony of anger. This is when a man starts to get angry at the world, angry for not delivering on its promises. You see, we were sold a bill of goods: if we worked hard, put our heads down, and were good guys, the world would give us everything we wanted. At the very least, we would get the love, respect, and admiration of the one person we wanted it the most from - our wife.

And when this doesn't pan out, we get angry. Angry that we feel like we are just a paycheck. We are just there to provide for our family and our wife as a means of making money. And out of this anger, we lash out at the ones closest to us. We lash out when we're not getting the respect we feel we deserve. We lash out when we realize we're not getting the sex we feel we deserve. We lash out when we don't get the love we feel we deserve. And when we lash out, we hurt those around us. We see the tears in their eyes and the hurt and disappointment on their faces.

And this brings in the third agony, the agony of shame. The agony of shame happens because we regret it when we turn to anger. We regret hurting the people around us even though we're hurting so much on the inside ourselves. The regret comes from hurting those around us and pushing them further and further away. And at times, we push them further away because we no longer want to hurt them. We no longer want to cause pain to those around us. We make up stories about how they would all be better off without us, and we beat ourselves up in unimaginable ways.

This brings us to the fourth agony, the agony of loneliness. And in No Man's Land, a man feels that he's by himself, often feeling like a lone wolf on the prairie.

No one understands his hardships, or perhaps no one cares. This is also why the second leading cause of death for men in Western society is suicide. A man often feels so lonely and ashamed for all the anger he's caused due to feeling empty that he takes his own life, and he does so out of this desperation. In this fourth agony, a man can be in a room full of people yet feel isolated and disconnected. He becomes lost, like a ship without a captain or port to dock.

This brings us to the fifth agony in No Man's Land. The agony of uncertainty. No longer is the world as clear-cut as it once was. Now the man doesn't know what's coming next. You see, many men who have strived for success and achieved it realize on the other side that they are coming home to their families as if they were strangers. They are uncertain if their marriages are going to last. They're uncertain if their kids actually love them. They are uncertain if the path that they're on will lead them to their dreams and their destination, out of No Man's Land. Typically, men at this stage will put their heads down and double down on work, where they at least know the rules of the game, hoping that something will change. Or they give up, thinking that this must be as good as it gets for me? A man wanders aimlessly through this period of his life and can wander along this path until he dies at the end of his days by natural causes or other means.

It's in No Man's Land that a man no longer feels like a man. He feels that no matter what he does, he's not making any progress. He's like a car stuck in the mud, and the harder he pushes his foot on the gas, the more the tires keep spinning and the deeper the car gets stuck. Some men continue to hit the gas, hoping that this time the car will finally get traction, but alas, the hole the tires are stuck in only gets deeper.

With no way out, the man is forced to throw up his hands and give up, live a life of quiet desperation, or find a way out—hopefully, one that results in him getting what he truly deserves.

I'm here to tell you that you can get unstuck and escape from No Man's Land. I've worked with thousands of men who have escaped, and the only thing that makes them unique is that they are committed to doing the work.

# The Sexless Marriage

Meet John. John had been married to his wife for 10 years, but for the past five, their relationship had become increasingly strained. They had always had a healthy and active sex life, but his wife recently lost all interest in physical intimacy.

John was confused and hurt by this sudden change. He tried talking to his wife about it, but she always brushed off his concerns and changed the subject. He even suggested couples therapy, but she wasn't interested. John felt like he was walking on eggshells in his own marriage, constantly worried about saying or doing the wrong thing that might further distance his wife from him.

He began to feel like he was in a sexless marriage, and it was taking a toll on his emotional and mental well-being. He missed the intimacy and connection that physical intimacy brought and longed for the closeness he and his wife once shared.

John didn't know what to do. He felt stuck in a situation that seemed to have no solution. He loved his wife but couldn't continue to live in a sexless marriage. He was at a loss as to how to move forward and was beginning to wonder if his marriage was worth saving.

I've worked with many men like John - sadly, his story is not uncommon at all.

When a relationship starts, sex is easy; it's effortless. You can't wait to rip each other's clothes off at a moment's notice. Given the space and the opportunity, you'll take any chance you get to go at it. You're both so turned on and tuned into each other that even unrealistic options start to look like possibilities. Sex at the office, sex at home, sex on the counter, sex in the car, sex while camping - sex just about anywhere. The passion is flowing between the two of you, and you can't keep your hands off each other.

But somewhere along the way, perhaps when children enter the picture, perhaps due to dramatic changes at work or moving, or simply because time passes, the sex dwindles and turns from a waterfall of sexual tension to a drip. this shifted the sex game from a daily activity to something you might do once a week to once a month. And for some of you, you haven't been intimate with your wife in several years. This is a tragedy, not only for you but also for her and for your marriage.

This drip can also dry up into what we call a "sexless marriage." It becomes easier and easier to push off having sex to the point where it just becomes plain difficult and feels awkward. And then sex starts to feel more like an obligation than something you're looking forward to. This all-too-familiar place that couples find themselves in is a place where you and your wife have grown distant and apart. So much so, that the analogy of having a roommate with a ring becomes dreadfully clear. You find yourself trying to meet your needs through alcohol, drugs, porn, prostitutes, escorts, or other women. Meanwhile, your wife lies only inches away from you in the bed or perhaps in the other room, yet it feels like she's miles away. You can reach out and touch her, if only you thought you could actually touch her without her pulling further away.

For many marriages, the dwindling desire seems to fall upon the wife. It seems as if it is she who is uninterested in having sex with her husband. She's not in the mood, or, in the classic example, she has a headache. Not tonight, dear, she says as she rolls over to sleep.

Meet Dave. At 39 years old, Dave was at the top of his game. His business was growing, and he was living his dream. The only thing that wasn't working for Dave was his sexless marriage. Dave found himself with his first child in a marriage, where it seemed like he and his wife argued about everything. These fights caused them to grow apart. To put out the fire, Dave started to placate and play nice to make things work. The sex went from a few times a week to a distant memory. Perhaps only when he and his wife would get drunk together would they fall into bed for a quick, unsatisfying sexual entanglement. Dave found himself searching porn sites more regularly. He'd get up early to go to his home office, only to find himself taking down his pants and searching on his favorite porn sites instead of getting the work done that sat in front of him (no pun intended, Dave).

Meanwhile, his wife lay in bed feeling distant, cold, and unwanted. She knew Dave must be jerking off to porn, or he had another woman on the side. She no longer felt desired. She no longer felt like a woman - at least not with Dave. Dave had given up, and it seemed like his wife had too.

Meet Craig. Craig, now in his mid-forties, is a successful entrepreneur with three lovely children that finds himself in the midst of a sexless marriage for the past two years. Craig can't even remember the last time he and his wife, Elizabeth, had sex. When first married, they had sex one to two times a day. It seemed like a never-ending love fest. Fast forward 10 years and three kids later, and Craig finds himself fantasizing about his interns and staff more than he thinks about his wife. He and his wife have become so cold and distant from each other that it's as if they're pretending to be married in front of the kids. As soon as the kids leave, their interactions become businesslike, working on logistics, who takes who to what practice, who makes lunches, and then they're off into their separate worlds. What Craig didn't know was that his wife was yearning for him to such an extent that she sought out another lover to fill the loneliness in their bedroom. Meanwhile, Craig is stuck in a sexless marriage, isolated, and lonely.

I could fill this entire book with stories like the ones above. Men who find themselves stuck in a sexless marriage. "I love my wife." They would all say. We just don't have sex.

The only difference between you and your wife's brother, cousin, or father is that you and your wife are intimate. Sure, she loves her brother and cousin. Yes, she's very close to her brother and cousin. Yes, she loves you or is very close to you. The difference is that a husband and wife are intimate - they have sex. And it's this intimacy that separates a husband and wife from two people who are just friends or close relatives. This is one reason intimacy is so vital to the health of a marriage.

And as the distance within the marriage grows to the point where it feels like you're six miles apart, even though you're lying six inches apart in bed, the rejection grows, and your wife begins to resent you for making advances on her. And it gets to the point where masturbation and pornography seem much easier.

This is also where another person can easily creep into the relationship, whether it be with you or with your wife.

As men, we seek sex to feel connected to our wives. This is a very primal thing. When we have sex, we feel closer and more in tune with our partner. Sex allows us to release pent-up energy and emotions. It's as if ejaculation is the release we need, and the space it creates allows for a deeper level of connection.

Whereas women need to feel connected to have passionate sex. The connection allows the woman to receive her man. Often, when I work with men who tell me their wife simply isn't sexual, it's really that she's not feeling connected to him. This lack of connection is also a major reason women turn outside of their marriages. Your wife needs to feel seen, heard, and desired to feel connected. We'll get more into that in the coming chapters.

You're aware that you're a sexual being, and you're aware that the barista at Starbucks, your secretary, or the woman at the gym who was paying you attention appears to be a simple conversion or at least an indication that you are desirable. Yet, for some reason, your wife is very distant. And the idea of you guys hooking up and having sex seems harder and harder, to the point where you no longer try. Because, let's face it, she's only going to reject you, and it's not going to turn out the way you want it to. And it's just going to be an obligation, which is just like masturbating anyway, except you'll be masturbating with a partner who's not interested. In that case, you still have to have the disappointment and the conversations that go along with it.

You are now just roommates, just friends, and you start to resent each other more over time.

Unbeknownst to you, your wife is most likely looking elsewhere for that companionship. She's still a very sexual being. It just so happens she's not sexually active with you.

Welcome to a sexless marriage, something that happens to more couples than you'll ever know. As a master coach with The Powerful Man, I hear a version of this story almost daily. My wife happens to coach women, so I also get to hear the other side of the story - the woman's side.

Sometimes I'll advise the husband while my wife works with his wife. Both parties are unhappy. Both parties are unfulfilled. And more often than not, their stories are riddled with blame and very different from their partners'. We also find that both parties often look to get their needs met elsewhere outside of the marriage, which can only be disastrous for everybody involved.

A sexless marriage is all too common. Yet, it's very rarely talked about. You have two people who love each other but haven't found a way to get back to one another romantically and sexually. Yes, it's one thing to have sex. But it's another thing to have passionate, connected sex that fills their needs physically, emotionally, and spiritually.

Many men find themselves in a situation where they start begging for sex, asking for blowjobs, and hoping their wives will take pity on them. They shower her with fancy gifts and do things around the house, only in the hopes of getting the sex that they want. Yet they find that this pity sex they are being given is completely unfulfilling.

Both parties leave the bedroom more distant and colder than they were before. This further entrenches the pattern of the sexless marriage to a point where neither couple can see a way out. Most men don't know that most online searches for how to stop or fix a sexless marriage are done by women, not men. This tells me that women are hoping, desiring, and wanting their men to step up and step in to end this drought. Women crave sex just as much as men. They want sex with their man in an intimate way. If not, they will seek someone else outside of the relationship.

When I speak to women about what we do at The Powerful Man to help husbands, they always ask how they can send their husbands our way. They don't do this because they hate him; they do it because they love him and are dying inside for their man to step to the line and break their cycle.

# Losing Respect and Power

Somewhere along the way, there was a power shift within your relationship. You started to lose power, or your wife started taking it from you. She had to.

She took it from you because she no longer trusted you. Over time, your wife started not respecting the choices and decisions that you were making. She no longer trusted that you could be the man that she thought you once were. This balance of power shifts because your wife needs to feel safe and secure, and she's no longer feeling that with you. So now she must take her safety and security into her own hands.

It's at this point when most men start to become the nice guy, and your wife starts becoming the Alpha. She needs to become the Alpha because she needs to know that she's safe, and because she no longer feels safe around you, whether emotionally, physically, or both, she needs to flip the script and take that power into her own hands. This usually begins with minor shittests, where she tests your resolve and mettle to see who you are.

Your wife often performs these tests, called "shittests," through manufactured complaints and manufactured problems. Often, she doesn't even know she's doing it. It happens naturally for her to ensure her safety and her family's safety.

Most men don't recognize these shittests for what they are, manufactured complaints designed to test your strength and resolve and actually think they are genuine grievances. Because they don't understand shittests, they cater to their women to keep her happy. Although noble and usually done out of love or to keep the peace, when they comply, they demonstrate to her that they lack power in the relationship.

Because they're giving their power away to their wife and doing whatever she wants rather than standing up for themselves, she now realizes that she has a dog and a pet, not a husband.

I know this is hard to hear. But this is the truth and reality that I had to face in order to save my own marriage.

I've heard someone explain this from an anthropological standpoint, which is that a woman must constantly test her mate to see how strong he is. The subconscious thought process is that if you can't stand up to her, how can you stand up to the caveman down the road who might come over and try to kill or rape her? Her life and the lives of her children depend on her husband being strong. Now, times have changed, and there isn't a saber-toothed tiger for you to protect her from, but the brain chemistry of humans hasn't changed, and therefore, she still must test your resolve.

When we react to these shittests, we're reacting to something outside of us, thus allowing whatever that thing is to control us.

If you can say something to make me angry and lose control, then you do, in fact, have control over me and my emotions. And to your wife, if she can make you react, then that means you can't control yourself, so how in the hell are you going to be able to handle her emotions?

She knows her emotions have wild ups and downs due to her hormonal cycles. If you can't handle that, then why should she allow herself to be free around you? And if she can't be free around you, well… you know the rest of that story.

This doesn't give you a license to be a jerk. You get to step up and be the leader you've always known yourself to be but simply lost along the way.

And when this power shifts, she is not only no longer going to trust you with her emotions, but she may also no longer trust you with decisions around money and may no longer trust you with decisions about your children.

She may even no longer trust you with straightforward decisions, such as your ability to grocery shop by yourself. This is emasculating, yet many men are so used to it, they just capitulate.

As absurd as this may sound. I've seen thousands of men battle with this loss of power and this transformation. Most of us surrender and figure it's easier to bite our tongue than to take on a verbal lashing from our wives.

Besides, if you do what she asks, then she'll be happy, things will work out, and you might even get laid, right? Wrong. We'll dive more deeply into this in the following chapter, but stay with me for now.

The funny thing is, women absolutely hate it when they have to take on the Alpha role. They don't want to be in power. They want a man they can trust fully, who can take control, and take the reins.

This is very obvious if you consider the book *50 Shades of Grey*, and the millions upon millions of copies of this book that were sold (150 million copies by 2017 alone). They sold so many copies of the book because of women's fantasies about having a man take control, with consent, and help them with their lives.

It's not that your wife can't do all of this herself, she can. A feminine woman, which most women fall into, needs a masculine man, or there is no polarity or attraction. Period.

Most married men have lost their power, and their wives have had to take over the Alpha role within the marriage, which leaves them feeling empty inside. Feminine energy naturally wants to remain in the feminine. It's where she's free and protected by a masculine source.

This is often why women have fantasies about firefighters, men in uniform, or their personal trainer at the local gym (trust me, I owned a gym and saw this often).

They fantasize about a man who appears to be in command of their life, or is on purpose, pursuing their destiny. And then they look at their husband, the man they once loved and admired, and wonder what happened to him. He has no control; he has no power.

She thinks, "All I have to do is tell him to do something, and he'll jump and do it." Or, "all I have to do is tell him I'm not happy, and he'll jump at my whim to try to make me happy."

This is akin to having a dog obey your commands and do whatever you want. This is not what women really want. Women want a man who has the power within them, keeps them in check when they test their resolve, and can rise up and respectfully put a woman in her place.

Even worse, many wives feel their husbands have become like big kids they have to take care of. Their husbands are always asking them for permission to do this or that. Just like her children, he seems helpless without her guidance. There is no place for her to let down her guard and surrender. At least the dog can do his own thing and not bother her all the time.

But for almost all marriages that I encounter during my work, the woman is wearing the pants in the family, and this is only because, as men, we haven't been taught how to respectfully take the power within our family and lead from the front to give the women in our lives the space that they need and that they deserve, so they may be fully present in and in their feminine energy.

Feminine energy is extremely powerful, and at the same time, as a masculine male, we slip into this feminine nature, which is unnatural for us. All of us have masculine and feminine energy, but for most men, we should be on the masculine side most of the time, thus allowing our women to be in a state of free-flowing feminine energy. This is where sexual energy is produced and where polarity is created.

Polarity creates sexual tension in a marriage and allows your wife to surrender into her feminine side. It will enable her to be in her true natural state, which is beautifully free-flowing… and she'll thank you for it. She's begging you for it. But unfortunately, most of us have fallen into the "nice guy" trap and given up our power to our wives. And reluctantly, they've taken that power because somebody has to be in control. Somebody has to take the power despite not wanting to; she needs to do it because the man in her life has not stepped up yet.

Let's take Dave, from the previous chapter, as an example.

The first several years of Dave's marriage were as expected - some ups and downs, but overall it was good. Then came the shift, or the pivot. Dave's wife started testing him to see if he could handle her. She didn't do this on purpose. Things had gotten a little stale; over time, she tested Dave more and more.

These tests started out as little upsets or complaints.

"You get to go out to these fancy work dinners while I'm at home with the kids! It's not fair!"

"You're going to work out again? I never have time for myself anymore."

Dave, like most nice guys, would feel guilty and react to what his wife was saying. He would defend his actions and then do whatever he could to solve her problems--often at the expense of himself.

Dave would stop going to the work dinners that had brought him in so much business and instead would start staying home to watch the kids so his wife could go out with her friends. He would trade in his workouts for her having more free time to do what she wanted to do.

Over time, Dave gave more and more of himself in the hope of making his wife happy. It didn't work.

# The Nice Guy - The Doormat

I get it. You're a nice guy. You don't want to hurt anyone. You want people to like you. Most of us do. In fact, what if I told you that you're pre-programmed to be a nice guy?

Your brain produces a hormone called serotonin. Serotonin's job is to help you climb the social ladder. Why? Because when we were on the plains of Africa, being alone meant almost certain death. If you twisted your ankle and were alone without anyone to help you, you were likely easy prey for another animal. By being a member of a tribe, your survival rate would be higher; as such, the higher your status within that tribe, the better access you would have to food, shelter, and mating. So, it stands to reason that if people don't like you, you're more likely to get kicked out of the tribe; thus, it's only natural to be a "nice guy" so you don't ruffle any feathers.

Your brain also produces a hormone called oxytocin. Oxytocin's job is to help you fall in love. When a child is born, the mother's body is flooded with oxytocin, and the bond formed between her and that child is unlike any other. As men, this also happens to us, but not to the same degree. The child needs the mother to survive. Our brains release oxytocin to help us bond with members of our tribe as well. Again, this is a survival mechanism.

Even though we are no longer on the African plains, that brain of yours that makes sense of the world is being controlled by the same drugs that ruled our forefathers centuries ago.

However, we're not in that society anymore. And the "nice guy" has officially become the doormat in modern society.

Now, when I say "nice guy," I'm not just talking about you being a good person. I'm going to take that as a default that we should all be good people, and we should all have some fundamental values of integrity, following the Golden Rule, do unto others as you'd have them do to yourself. This is why almost all religions share 90% of the same tenets as their primary ways of being a good human. However, the "nice guy syndrome" is different.

And most men have fallen into "nice guy" syndrome, regardless of their station in life and physical prowess. Robert Glover talks about this in more detail in his book, "*No More Mr. Nice Guy*. I recommend grabbing a copy if you want to learn more.

These "nice guys" get taken advantage of by other men and also by women.

In my experience, most nice guys "lone wolf it" because they don't trust people anymore. Their wives and girlfriends have cheated on them, and their friends have taken and stolen money from them. And they don't trust people anymore because they've been hurt so often. So often, they've been willing to give the shirt off their back, only to find out that the person they gave it to has been hoarding shirts for years and has no intention of returning the favor.

In your marriage, you become the nice guy to appease your wife, thinking that if you can make her happy, your marriage will be successful. You haven't just done this for sex, but let's be real, you've done it at times in the hopes of getting laid.

Really, you're acting out this "nice guy" persona because you want your wife to be happy. You want your wife to think of you as a great man, a good husband, and a great father.

Chances are that you are a great guy.

However, that nice guy becomes a doormat, then a whipping boy, and then the dog of the family.

It starts with small requests and then those requests start to increase more and more.

You start to fail these shittests that your wife will give to see if you're strong enough to protect her, and you start to think of them as genuine requests or real complaints rather than manufactured ones, which tests are designed to do, and you answer the call.

By reacting to her tests, you're showing her that you're not strong enough to handle her, let alone strong enough to handle the caveman down the way, and you, therefore, can't protect her. So she steps on you some more to see if you're really as weak as you appear to be.

Being a nice guy, you decide to comply to make her happy. And although she asked for it, this is not what she ever wanted.

You find yourself doing more chores around the house, giving up on your dreams, your passions, and your hobbies to allow her to have hers, staying at home doing chores around the garden, and hanging out with friends that you don't even care about, all to appease everybody.

Sadly, often when a man has been a "nice guy" for a long time, he finds out that his wife is having an emotional or physical affair.

This isn't even the most shocking part for most men. They are taken aback when they learn about the man she is with.. He's rarely more successful, rarely better looking, rarely has better physical prowess, or makes more money. He usually happens to be a jerk.

The difference between the man she's having an affair with and the man that she's married to is that the man she's having an affair with is not a doormat, or at least not in their limited interactions, he has not been perceived to be a doormat. Chances are, he does not care about her the way that you do. And because you care so much, you've allowed her to step all over you because of the thought that you are a nice guy, and this is what love is about - compromise.

It was an illusion. Being a doormat and doing whatever your partner says is not an expression of love. This is not what being a good man is about. A good man is a powerful man. And we'll go over what that means in greater detail in subsequent chapters.

Dave did this exact thing. In an effort to regain his wife's love and admiration, Dave doubled down on being a "Nice Guy." He bit his tongue when she put him down or simply was out of line. He didn't want to rock the boat; even more so, Dave thought that if he was just a better husband, she would see how amazing he was and want to be intimate.

Dave would come home early from work to allow her more free time away from the kids. He'd clean the house while she was away so that she didn't have that burden. Dave would even work on the weekends so he could take her on expensive trips, rather than taking time to rest or do things he loved. Dave had become a "Nice Guy" and a doormat.

# Hiding Out & Sedation

A long your journey in this game we call life, the world beats you up, knocks you down, and sometimes you stumble to get back up, only to be slapped back down to the ground again.

As these trials and tribulations continue to beat us down, many men begin to hide out in sedation. We start hiding out in our own little worlds, and many men do this differently.

It often starts out fairly young and suddenly grows to the point where we start to create our little fantasy world. Or we hide our true selves, attempting to mold ourselves to fit the group agenda.

This is especially true in dysfunctional households where you were taught to behave in certain ways as a survival mechanism. Some of us used our intellect and got good grades, while others learned to keep quiet and not draw attention to themselves. Still others took on the role of the hero and worked to help everyone, only to feel let down because we could never help "everyone." These are all coping mechanisms, and so is sedation.

Consider sedation as turning off the world, your thoughts, and your emotions. You're just there, but it's not the whole you that's there. Sedation isn't about being present; in fact, it's the exact opposite of being present. You're using something to escape reality.

When we sedate ourselves and hide out, we really give up our power, not only to our wives but also to society.

We begin to dim our light so that others can shine brighter. We hide the greatness inside us, and instead of stepping to the line and showcasing the amazing men we are, we stuff that man down and hide him from the world.

We dim our light in front of our wives because perhaps we've been too successful in business. We don't want her to feel bad that maybe she hasn't had that level of success.

Perhaps we've been too successful in athletics, so we allow others to win out of pity for them or because we don't want them to feel bad. Worse, we may self-sabotage, so we don't stand out.

From what I've seen, men who are afraid of cheating often stop working out, eat badly, and gain weight to make it less likely that other women will find them attractive, which makes them less likely to cheat. Crazy right? Yet we do this in many areas of our lives.

Perhaps our children really enjoy playing with us more than they do with their mother. So we dim our light so our wife feels better. We don't want our wife to feel bad about the kids choosing us over her. I've caught myself doing this many times. It doesn't serve my wife, the kids, or me. There are much better ways to "be" that serve everyone.

Men frequently sedate themselves and hide out in sedation because they don't want to face the ugly facts and things aren't going their way. Perhaps things aren't working out in their business, perhaps they're not working out in their marriage, or perhaps their body isn't the way they want it to be. Perhaps it is something else. Either way, it's the act of hiding out that really makes us play small.

Some men sedate themselves through porn. Sex starts happening less and less frequently. Their fantasies aren't being met by their wives. Most likely, they're too scared to talk to their wife about their fantasies. "What will she think of me? What will she say if she finds out that this is something I'm interested in? She'll never like it. She'll never go for it. She'll judge me."

And so we hide out, often thinking, "You know what, she's just gonna say no if I ask her to have sex, or it's just too much work; therefore, I'll go ahead and just watch porn and jerk off instead." We sedate ourselves, thus contributing to making the sexless marriage, or the time between sexual escapades in the bedroom even further and further apart. Getting what we think is fulfilling our needs through masturbation when it often leaves us feeling good for a moment but quickly fading.

To top it off, studies have shown that masturbation actually lowers testosterone, whereas having sex and intercourse can increase it. (If you've fallen into the Nice Guy Syndrome or find yourself in DEER mode (chapter 8), then you might want to look into raising your testosterone, not lowering it.)

Men also hide out through the use of alcohol and drugs. Often, we've seen the scene where a man comes home after a busy day of work, the kids are screaming, and his wife is standing in the room looking miserable. And so he pours a healthy glass of bourbon or scotch to numb the pain.

One glass becomes two, and two becomes three. Eventually, this routine becomes a habit or ritual. That routine and habit also allow us to be tripped up, losing control of our thoughts and emotions. We lash out at our wives at the worst possible times, causing more problems and drama than we need. This outburst then puts us right into the guilt and shame loop, where we feel guilty and ashamed of the way we acted, for making our wife cry and for not being a good enough man. Thus, we jump right back into "nice guy" mode again, but this time we work at it twice as hard, only to get worse results than before.

Men will also keep themselves from pursuing their goals and dreams by gambling, playing video games, or just watching TV and sports. This is all too common in Western society. where men had been stuck in this Neverland boy syndrome for far too long, coming home after work, having some drinks, throwing on the TV, and sitting on the couch. And as time passes, our wife becomes increasingly estranged from us.

Maybe she's joining you on the couch, sedating herself as well. Or maybe she's off doing something else. Or maybe she's on her phone, DMing an ex with the fantasy that things could have been better or different if she had married someone else.

This is an all-too-common scene in households across the world. And unfortunately, the remedy is taking massive action, which can be very hard. As I always say, you get to choose your "hard," because being in a sexless marriage that's tearing apart your soul is also hard.

Which "hard" will you choose?

It's hard to change. I get it. You're preprogrammed to stay the same. Your ego says, "Hey, things suck, but we're alive, and my job is to keep you alive, so let's not rock the boat, and instead, let's keep things the way they are."

It's our ego's job to protect us. It will come up with all kinds of reasons why you shouldn't take action. It will tell you it's too hard. It will tell you it will never work. It will tell you that it's not worth the risk. It's not the right time; if you just wait, things will get better on their own.

The excuses are endless, but the end result is always the same: you get inspired to change because you know it's the best move, and then you do nothing because that's the safe thing to do. And you stay in the same place you are today - not horrible, but also not happy.

But in my opinion, it's harder to live an average or below-average life. You were meant for greatness. The mathematical odds of you being here are $10^{2,685,000}$ (For those unfamiliar with scientific notation, that number is a 10 followed by almost 2.7 million zeros).

Would you bet on those odds in Vegas? Of course not, yet you're here. If this number throws you off due to your religious beliefs, then let me ask you this respectfully, would God want you to live an average life?

It's going to be hard regardless of whether you stay the same or if you choose to change. Choose your "hard."

Sedation is simply putting a bandaid on the issue.

An analogy I like to use is this:

Imagine you were walking out the front door of your home. As you pass the door frame, a nail sticking out cuts you in the arm, and you say, "Ow, that hurts!" And so you go back into the house and into the bathroom, put a bandaid on it, and go about your day to stop the bleeding.

The next day, you walk out the door again. "Ouch, that hurts!" You say, as you cut yourself again on the same nail. So what do you do? You get another bandage to put on the cut, this time over the one you had on before.

This goes on day after day until the scar on your arm gets stronger and stronger. Cutting yourself as you walk out the door just becomes a thing you do; it's no longer a big deal. It's just what you do.

What I'm going to teach you to do in this book, in relation to your marriage, is to ditch the bandaid (what you're doing now in your marriage) and instead, go into your garage, grab a pair of pliers, and rip that friggin nail out once and for all (do the work).

It's not as easy as putting a bandaid on because that nail's in there deep. But if you're determined and give it all you have, then once you rip that nail out, you don't have to worry about cutting yourself again. This is what it's like to break the pattern of sedation.

Now, I'm not suggesting that you don't use porn, you don't have a drink, and you don't play video games, or watch a movie. I'm suggesting that when you choose to do these things, you do so with intent. I'm suggesting you do it consciously. I'm suggesting you don't make it a pattern that stops you from shining as brightly as you possibly could, Brother. You do this through a place where you gain control and get the optics that you need so that you can continue to grow.

The world needs more great men. My secret plan in writing this book is to help you with your marriage so that you can be one of the great men out there, making this world a better place for your family and mine. You simply can't do that if you're constantly sedating yourself.

When we look back at our friend Dave, he would cope with his newfound life by pouring a cocktail as soon as he got done with work. One cocktail turned into two, and two turned into five. Dave knew he wasn't going to be having sex at night, so he would turn on a movie or the game as soon as he got done helping out around the house. His routine became so well known to his family that it was simply thought of as "that's what Dave does."

As the weeks, months, and years passed, Dave started to put on more and more weight. He became less and less interested in doing other things with his friends or his family. At one point, Dave saw himself in a photo from a family event and could barely recognize the man in the picture. "What happened?" he thought to himself. "This isn't the life I wanted. Where'd all the time go?" Dave was hiding out in sedation… killing time… and himself.

# The DEER and The WOLF

When I'm walking through the woods, I often stumble upon deer. When they see me, they become skittish.

They pop up their heads, and they watch my every move, reacting to everything I do. And one perceived aggressive gesture by me sends the deer running as fast as they can, heading for the hills, heading for safety.

This is not unlike what happens in a marriage.

At The Powerful Man, we use DEER as an acronym for Defend, Excuse, Explain, React. When a man gets married and things start to get tough, men tend to become deactivated over time and go into "nice guy" mode, which we talked about in a previous chapter. They become the deer in their marriage.

Along the journey of a sexless marriage, most men have been taught that the way to gain their wife's love, admiration, and respect again is to be a nicer guy.

And in order to be a nicer guy, they end up biting their tongue, swallowing their pride, and not standing up for themselves because they don't want to upset the apple cart and cause drama or waves in the marriage. As a result, they suppress their emotions and upsets.

When things do come up in the marriage, they find themselves instantly reacting to their wife's mood or what they believe to be their wife's attack on them. They defend their actions, and they explain why they did what they did or why they are doing what it is that they are doing, and then they make excuses for what they are doing or have already done.

This immediately puts them on their heels and puts them into victim mode, the victim mode of the deer. So let's break this down and also break down what it means to be a wolf, the opposite of the deer, and something that you felt before in your life but somehow has escaped you.

In "DEER", the letter "D" stands for "defend." As men, we tend to defend our actions or defend the things that we say, as if we are on trial in a courtroom and need to justify our actions, our words, or our emotions. It's in this defending that we are communicating that we are subservient to the other person. Now, this isn't always the case, but when you're emotionally reacting to a situation and find yourself defending against an accusation with energy, you're telling the other person that they have the power, and you need to explain yourself to them.

This isn't the path of the wolf, and this also isn't sexy to your wife.

An example of this might be if you decided to go golfing with your buddies on a Saturday, and you come home to find your wife upset because the trash wasn't taken out, the dishes weren't done, or the lawn wasn't mowed.

Let's also assume that doing these chores was never agreed upon by you and your wife. Yet, you immediately start defending the fact that you have the right to go out with your buddies because, hey, she went out with her girlfriends last week as well.

We instantly go into this defensive mode, which then means our wife is the aggressor or the alpha in this situation. Because we react, which is the R in DEER, to her accusations, this not only shows that her accusations have merit, but that they also carry weight with us. Thus, by defending ourselves, it also showcases that she has the power.

We then explain and make excuses about how we don't get time to spend with our friends, and that's not fair. We explain that we were now going to take out the trash (or mow the lawn or whatever else the accusation may be) or how it wasn't our responsibility, once again giving up all the power to our partners.

When we enter DEER mode, we immediately become children, defending our actions and attempting to explain why we did what we did and why it wasn't wrong. This showcases the power dynamic of our wife, the person who's in charge and us being subservient to her. This is not sexy.

Do you remember that movie where all the women fight with each other to sleep with the guy who comes to their beck and call and answers their every wish and desire? No, me neither, because they never made that movie because that's not what women want and deep down, we know it.

It's not your fault that men have been socialized to go into DEER mode. It's been beaten into you at a young age.

However, every time you go into DEER mode with your partner, she becomes more alpha. This is not the natural state of feminine energy. Feminine energy wants to be wild and free. It wants to be safe within a container it knows can protect her.

Feminine energy thinks: If you can't protect yourself from me, how can you protect me from the outside world, from the caveman down the street, or from any other intrusion that's coming into our lives? If you can't handle your wife, how can you protect her?

This is what happens whenever we go into DEER mode. We further stack evidence for our partner that we can't be trusted. We can't be trusted to be powerful, and thus, we can't be trusted to catch them when they fall, metaphorically speaking.

Women often talk about wanting a man who's strong enough to handle them. And when a man is strong enough to handle them, they will submit to that man by choice. By choice and by love, respect, and admiration. This is not a path of force but a path of surrender.

Remember, the deer, as nice as they may be, are still the prey and at the bottom of the food chain.

DEER

D - Defend: When you react to what your wife says, especially during a shittest, and defend your actions as if you have to explain yourself to her. She's the boss, and you're the employee.

E - Explain: When you follow up a shitest by explaining in detail why you did what you did. Again, you are doing this out of fear of what she might say or do, and since you don't want to piss her off, you explain to her why you did what you did.

E - Excuse: This occurs when you feel you have to make excuses for your actions. It wasn't your fault after all. You explain to her why she shouldn't be upset with you or scold you like a bad boy.

R - React: This is when you react to something your wife says. When you react, this shows she has power over you. Don't believe me? Imagine I come up to you and say you're purple. Chances are you'd look at me oddly. For starters, you don't believe you're purple, so it doesn't bother you, hence no reaction. Chances are you wouldn't know it was me, the man in your corner, so you would just stare at me blankly and tell me to walk away. The reason you're able to stay so stoic in these situations is because I have no control over you. When you react to your wife, you're showing her that she does, in fact, have control over you. Don't do it.

Now, enter the wolf.

WOLF is an acronym for Wise, Open, Loving, and Fierce.

A powerful man possesses all these characteristics. In this book, we've talked about how the feminine needs the masculine to act as a container so it can fully express itself. Being the wolf allows your wife to feel safe, secure, and surrender to you. When this occurs, she will not only feel safe, but she will also feel energetically attracted to you.

Picture two super magnets, each five feet tall. When you turn those magnets so that their polarity is the same direction when they face each other, then no amount of force can bring them together. This is what has happened in most modern marriages. You are most likely a naturally masculine man, and your wife, a naturally feminine woman, has felt the need to take on and express her masculine side, thus causing the two of you to repel each other. This is because modern society has deactivated you--you've become a shell of your former self within your marriage.

Now, let's take those same two super magnets and turn one of them around so that the polarity of the magnetic field is opposite. The magnets not only attract each other, but you'd have a difficult time taking those magnets apart. This occurs when you become "activated" and embrace the WOLF.

Let's break down each characteristic of the wolf.

The "W" is for the word "Wise." A wolf is always growing, not unlike you reading this book, and he leans on his experience to navigate the world. The wolf doesn't allow himself to get "triggered," or said another way; the wolf doesn't react to outside influences and easily get flustered. Instead, he practices engaged indifference. He chooses his responses.

Engaged indifference is the art of being engaged in a conversation or in the moment while also being indifferent to the outcome. This is a very stoic stance on life.

As an example, I can walk up to my wife and give her a big kiss, while still being indifferent to her response. Not only does this give me the power to do what I want when I want since I'm not afraid of rejection, but it also turns my wife on because I'm leading and following my purpose (thus being activated).

I want to be crystal clear here - I'm not doing anything that would be deemed as violating my wife. That's not what we're talking about. There are times when my wife is upset with me and may not want me to touch her, and I respect her wishes when she expresses them to me. However, if she's simply upset and hasn't requested a boundary, then I do what feels right to me in the moment without worrying about how she might react. I'm respectful, but not scared or intimidated.

Another example of where engaged indifference comes in handy is when your wife pulls a shittest on you. You can sit in the eye of the storm, look at her lovingly, and not react to what she's saying. The ability to do this will show your wife that you can handle yourself and her.

Like many of the skills in this book, engaged indifference needs to be practiced for the deactivated man, but through practice comes mastery, and through mastery comes the wisdom of the wolf.

The "O" in WOLF stands for "Open." The wolf opens himself up to the world. He is no longer scared of being hurt, attracted, or betrayed because he knows that all he needs is inside him. He is activated and is now back in the driver's seat of his life. And because he knows that no one can emotionally hurt him, he can be his true self around others and shine his light brightly upon the world.

Women will often say that there's nothing sexier than a confident man who doesn't care what others think of him. This is why sometimes you may see a man that you feel is beneath your station in life, looks, and wealth, yet he is with an amazing woman. This man is activated, and she knows it. His stock is high in her eyes, and she knows that it will not crash regardless of how much money he makes or how he looks. His heart is open, and thus she can feel him. A woman cannot connect with a man who has closed his heart to the world.

I recall when my wife told me that closing myself off to her was more painful than if I had actually physically abused her. As a man raised on the principle that you never hit a woman, and I haven't, this shocked me. I'm not a small guy, so if I were to hit my wife (again, I never have and never will), then it would cause serious damage. So, for my wife to tell me that she'd rather I hit her than shut down emotionally was very eye-opening for me, and since that comment, I've confirmed her sentiment with hundreds of women.

Closing down makes us less open to receiving and thus makes it harder for people to connect with us, including our wives. By being open, you're basically saying, "Look here, world, I'm strong enough to handle anything you're throwing my way; if you want to throw something my way, I can take it because you cannot hurt me." And the truth is, the world cannot.

A powerful man is solid in his foundation. He's activated, meaning he finds all the power within himself. And thus, he can be open and brave. And when attacks come, they can still hurt, but he also knows he can handle that pain and make it through to the other side.

When a man knows he can handle any possible pain, it allows him to connect to the marrow of life and allows him to connect to all the greatness around him. It allows him to experience all the colors of the rainbow rather than just a few select ones and live a mundane life.

Openness also shows your heart to your partner and allows her to see the true you and feel safe to show you all of her - including her freaky side in the bedroom, but that's just a side benefit many men report. Because once you feel safe with yourself as the wolf, now she can feel safe with you.

Has your wife ever mentioned wishing you were more open? Or perhaps she's made comments about you being closed down?

Many of us close our hearts to the world as a result of being hurt, attacked, or shunned. It's a defense mechanism that starts at a very young age for a man. Real men don't cry, right?

Wrong. The truth is that being vulnerable without fear is a true example of courage, not hiding yourself from the world. Courage, after all, is defined by being afraid and doing something anyway. We say the fireman who runs into the burning house to save a child is courageous.

Why? Because he went into that house despite being afraid of what might happen to him.

Opening your heart is the most courageous thing a man can do. This is the path of the wolf.

The "L" in WOLF is for "Loving." We're all in search of love. We're in search of being loved by others, and you wouldn't be reading this book if you weren't in search of winning your wife's love back. When you look at the logo for The Powerful Man, it's a wolf with a rose in his mouth, showcasing the power of the teeth and the tenderness of his love.

A powerful man does not hold back his love. He does not trade his love as if it were some sort of transactional deal. "I'll open my heart and show you how much I love you, but only when I know you'll love me back and won't reject me. You first."

What many men forget is that love is abundant. You can't give too much love away. In fact, the more love you give, the more you get.

Don't believe me?

When you had your first child, did your love diminish or grow? It grew, right? Well, when you loved this new being, did you lose love for your wife at that time? Probably not. How about your second child? Did you have to divide your love 50/50 or 40/60 and pick which child got a certain amount of love, or did your love simply expand?

For some reason, society has conditioned us as men to withhold our love. It's as if we only had a certain amount, and only certain people were worthy of that love. If I give my love to someone and they don't reciprocate, then I somehow lose out.

That's a scarcity mindset and the mindset of the deer. Somewhere along our journey, we became deactivated and thus withheld our love from people as a weird form of manipulation.

No more. Your eyes are becoming more open, my friend. You're starting to see the playing field for what it is. I wish you the opportunity to attend an Alpha Reset, a four-day event put on by The Powerful Man that strips these blinders off a man. I'm not sharing this with you as a pitch. My life won't change if you go or don't, but yours will.

The loving nature of the world allows a man to give and receive gratitude for things around him. The wolf is strong, and the loving side of him brings out his playful side and fun nature.

If you watch nature documentaries, you'll often see little pups jumping all over the Alpha male, playing and nipping at him, all because they can sense his power and love. They are safe.

When I embraced the wolf and became "activated," I would practice loving all the people I would interact with--at the grocery store, while in line, and at work. The response I got back from people filled my soul. And when I practiced this with my wife, I could see the stress and anxiety melt away.

But we know the wolf isn't some sort of hippie dancing in the fields. No. The "F" in WOLF is for "Fierce."

Yes, he is wide, open, and loving. But the wolf can also be fierce.

At a moment's notice, the wolf can show his power and let his strength be known. The wolf uses his ability to be fierce to protect his wife, his kids, and those things that mean the most to him.

Our society looks down upon men who are strong. I think this is sad. As a man, you have more testosterone than your wife, and as such, you have the ability to be stronger. That's an amazing attribute that you get to tap into. This doesn't give you a license to be a jerk-- remember, the wolf is also open and loving. However, as the old saying goes, it's better to be a warrior in a garden than a gardener in a war.

Many of the men that come into the Powerful Man movement take up martial arts. They don't do this to fight. In fact, I can't recall one man who's been in a fight that I'm aware of. These powerful men practice the fighting arts to tap into their natural state, the fierceness of the wolf.

Being fierce gives you a license to stand up for yourself, stand up for what you believe in, and protect those things that matter most to you. If this is your marriage, you must protect your marriage against yourself and against your wife and any outside intruders. These outside intruders could be society, drugs, addictions, other men, or anything that's going to be toxic and make your marriage more difficult than it needs to be.

The wolf is far superior to the deer, and your wife is looking for a wolf. This is often the case when you see women fantasizing through books or movies about the strong, independent character out there leading the world. (Do you think James Bond is a deer or a wolf?)

Books and movies are written to appeal to our inner desires--that's why we watch them. Writers of romance novels and action movies often have a lead character who possesses the traits of the WOLF. The lead character goes out into the world, fighting for what he believes in with passion and strength. When he comes home, he's nurturing and loving. He takes care of his family and those around him. Although he spends most of his time with a loving and peaceful energy, he can turn on his aggression like a switch when he needs to protect his family from evil forces.

I highly recommend getting a wolf logo or wolf statue to put on your desk at work and somewhere in your home to remind you of who you get to be so that you may become the man you've always seen when you look in the mirror. I myself have a large poster in my office that I look at as soon as I walk into the room, and it serves as a reminder to be wise, open, loving, and fierce.

I'll put several images the men we've worked with use on the website: www.ThePowerfulMan.com/book.

As time went on, Dave's wife grew further and further away. When she challenged Dave's actions, he would immediately react and defend himself. It wouldn't be a normal reaction, either. Dave had pushed down all the resentment from all the times he bit his tongue or felt he wasn't respected or treated fairly. He was, after all, a nice guy, and nice guys don't yell--until they explode.

Dave's eruptions would start with a reaction and immediately follow with him explaining why he had done what he had done, defending himself as if he were under attack. All the buildup inside Dave would come out, and it wasn't pretty.

Dave's wife would cry and the distance between them would become greater. Dave would end up feeling more guilty than before and mad, this time, at himself. He was slipping deeper into his shadow.

# The Shadow

Welcome to the chapter on the shadow stickman. This concept is important to understand if you are looking to save your marriage and improve your relationships. But what is the shadow stickman, and why is it so important?

The shadow stickman represents the unconscious aspects of a person's personality. It includes both positive and negative qualities that the individual is not fully aware of or does not accept about themselves. The shadow stickman can often manifest as defensive or negative behaviors in relationships, and it can be a major barrier to achieving true intimacy and connection with your partner.

By understanding and identifying your "shadow stickman," you can gain greater self-awareness and learn how to navigate the challenges that arise in your marriage. In this chapter, we will delve into what the shadow stickman is, how to identify it, and how to work with it to improve your relationship. Let's get started.

The shadow stickman is a critical concept in psychology, particularly in Jungian psychology, and it is seen as an important part of the psyche.

Jungian psychology helps people understand themselves better by exploring their inner thoughts and feelings. It suggests that everyone has an inner self that affects their behavior and personality, including their relationships with others. For a man trying to save his marriage, understanding his own inner thoughts and feelings can help him identify and address any issues that may be affecting his relationship. By exploring his own inner self and working to improve his communication and understanding with his partner, he can work towards rebuilding and strengthening his marriage.

In relationships, the shadow stickman can often manifest as defensive or negative behaviors. For example, if you have a tendency to become angry or defensive when you feel criticized by your partner, this could be a manifestation of your shadow stickman. Similarly, if you find yourself engaging in behaviors that are self-sabotaging or that hurt your relationship, this could also be a sign of the shadow stickman at play.

It's important to note that the shadow stickman is not necessarily a negative or "bad" thing. It is a part of the unconscious psyche and can include both positive and negative qualities. The key is to become aware of and understand the shadow stickman so that you can work with it rather than letting it dictate your behavior in your relationships.

How to identify the shadow stickman:

One of the first steps to working with the shadow stickman is to become aware of its presence. Here are some tips for identifying the shadow stickman in your own life:

Pay attention to your reactions and behaviors in difficult situations or conflicts with your partner. Notice if you tend to get defensive or if you do things that hurt others or hurt yourself. These can be signs of the shadow stickman at play.

Notice patterns of behavior that you may not be fully aware of. Do you tend to react in a certain way in certain situations? Do you have a pattern of avoiding certain topics or behaviors with your partner? These patterns may be influenced by the shadow stickman.

Reflect on any negative or self-sabotaging thoughts or beliefs that may be contributing to these behaviors. For example, do you have a belief that you are not good enough or that you are unworthy of love? These types of beliefs can be a sign of the shadow stickman at work.

Identifying the shadow stickman can be a challenging process, but it is an essential step in improving your relationships and achieving greater self-awareness. By paying attention to your reactions, behaviors, and thoughts, you can begin to understand what makes up your shadow stickman and how it may impact your life.

Working with the shadow stickman:

Once you have identified the shadow stickman and have a better understanding of its influence on your behavior and relationships, you can begin the process of working with it.

Here are some steps to consider:

Acknowledge and accept the existence of the shadow stickman. This is an important first step, as it allows you to approach the shadow stickman with curiosity and openness rather than resistance or denial.

Reflect on the positive and negative qualities that make up your shadow stickman and how they may impact your relationship. Take some time to journal or reflect on these qualities and how they manifest in your life.

Seek support and guidance. Working with the shadow stickman can be a challenging process, and it can be helpful to seek the support of a therapist or other professional to help guide you through it. There are also many self-help resources available that can provide guidance on this process.

By taking these steps and working with the shadow stickman, you can gain greater self-awareness and improve your relationships. It's not always an easy process, but it can lead to greater fulfillment and happiness in your life.

Understanding and working with the shadow stickman is important in improving your relationships and achieving greater self-awareness. By becoming aware of the unconscious aspects of your personality and learning how to navigate their influence on your behavior, you can create healthier, more fulfilling relationships.

It's not always an easy process, but it is a worthwhile one. By acknowledging and accepting the shadow stickman, reflecting on its qualities, and seeking support and guidance, you can integrate this aspect of your psyche into your conscious identity.

# Making the Shift

People often ask me why I still choose to lead live events. There are many reasons, but one of the biggest reasons is that I get to see the exact moment when a man shifts from deactivated to activated. If you've watched the *Matrix* movies, you'll recall that moment when Keanu Reeves' character, Neo, gets unplugged from the matrix. Neo goes on to not only realize that he's been in a simulation (deactivated) but then gets to master the real world and become what we call ""activated.""

Making the shift from what you've been doing to where you want to be isn't easy, but as I said earlier, you get to choose your hard. Which one will you choose?

Make that decision now. This isn't something to take lightly. The number one thing I hear previously from men who have gone through this process when I ask them what advice they would give to their former self is "Do this sooner." I hear this every time. Not most of the time, but every time.

When you start to shift and change the way you show up in the world, you can expect to meet some resistance. As hard as it may be to hear, you've taught the people around you how to treat you and how to act toward you. In this same light, you've taught them how to think of you. This is most evident for men when they go home and change how they act in front of their childhood family, whom they don't see very often. We fall back into roles that we've had for decades. Or perhaps you see an old friend you haven't seen in a long time and fall right back into roles you had previously played or thoughts about who they are, even though years have gone by and they may have changed.

You will most likely meet resistance along the way.

Take this resistance as a good sign. This means people are starting to notice you're changing. Why is this good? Well, because you're not going to get where you want to go by showing up in the world the way you're currently showing up, or you wouldn't be reading this book. Just like an alcoholic needs to make a clear, "burn the boats," type of decision to stop drinking to get sober, you must also make that level of commitment to doing whatever it takes to become the wolf and to become activated.

It's common for men who join the Activation Method, our eight-week flagship program, to hit resistance for the first few weeks of the program. It's also common for them to turn their marriages around after only a few weeks.

Sure, they stumble and fall. These are new skills you're learning, and the odds are that you might not be doing them perfectly at first. Also, your wife is still expecting the old you to appear, and when you appear as the man she's always wanted to be with, she'll be excited and then terrified that it won't last... that she'll be hurt again.

This is why you need to commit to going all in. We call this "stepping to the line" in The Powerful Man movement.

Again, you won't get everything right the first time. In fact, it takes about 64 repetitions of use of a new skill to build the neural pathway in a way that feels comfortable and natural. On your path to mastery, you must put in your reps. Having a coach is the absolute best way to do so, but short of that, use this book as your coach, and when you stumble, pick yourself up and keep going.

Have you made your commitment? If so, then let's get into some of the methodologies that will allow you to be successful.

Dave's shift was initially very subtle. He woke up one morning and walked into the bathroom to brush his teeth. When he looked into the mirror, he saw a man who looked far older than he was, had put on weight, and Dave started thinking about why he should even be here on this planet anymore. It was at that moment that Dave decided that something had to change.

Dave knew that his wife was more like a roommate with a ring than the passionate lover he had married so many years ago. He knew that he loved his kids and didn't want to break up his family, but at the same time, he wondered if life was really worth living anymore.

Dave had hit a turning point and he was ready to make a shift. "What I'm doing just isn't working, so what's the risk in trying something different?" Dave thought to himself.

This thought was the first step to making the shift for Dave and for many men like him. You have to be willing to make a change, to go all in, before a change can actually occur.

# The Triad of Connection

To make the shift, you need a set of tools. A doctor has a stethoscope and a scalpel. A carpenter has a hammer and a level, and to make the shift from a sexless marriage to one where your wife is looking at you with love, respect, and admiration once again, you need what we call "the Triad of Connection."

The Triad of Connection is a set of three tools developed by The Powerful Man for our flagship program, The Activation Method.

If you can picture a triangle, as a triangle has three sides, these three tools come together to complete this triad. One of those tools is the Clean Slate Method, which allows you to "wipe the slate clean" and start from scratch in your relationship.

This is analogous to taking an eraser to a metaphorical whiteboard with all the negative experiences and feelings in your relationship written down on it

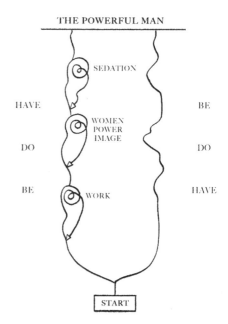

and then using the Clean Slate Method to wipe them all off. You are then left with a clean, empty whiteboard, from which you can create anything you want.

With the Clean Slate Method, you not only get to bring the scales back from being heavily weighted with negative thoughts and feelings to being balanced and neutral, but you get to draw a line in the sand that clearly marks a new starting point.

Now, although getting the scales in your relationship back to neutral is going to feel amazing, it's not where we want to stop. We want to make sure those good experiences far outweigh the negative ones, so the scale tips in your favor. And for that, we use a process we call the Hidden Motives Technique.

The Hidden Motives Technique is another tool in The Triad of Connection that is going to allow your wife to be seen and heard, probably for the first time in your relationship.

I know that sounds crazy, but we hear this from men every single day at The Powerful Man, where their wives will tell them that they've never felt closer to their husbands as they have when that man's been using the Hidden Motives Technique. It draws your wife in toward you naturally and effortlessly. The scales are now tipped back in your favor, with the good feelings far outweighing the bad ones.

Of course, we don't want to stop there because we don't want the scales to tip back out of your favor. We want them to stay in your favor for as long as you desire, which I will assume is forever. And that's where the third part of the Triad of Connection comes in.

We call this third part the Live Like a King System.

The Live Like a King System allows you to keep those scales tipped in your favor, where the good experiences and feelings far outweigh the bad ones for the duration of your relationship and beyond. You can think of the Live Like a King System as a brake that prevents the scales from tipping back out of balance, as long as you consistently use the other two sides of the triad together.

The Live Like a King System is a series of activities that you'll be able to do that will reinforce the behavior patterns that allow you to be the powerful man you've always been inside. It will prevent you from slipping back into DEER mode and allow you to embrace further the lifestyle of the wolf - being wise, open, loving, and fierce.

These three tools will be the basis of your toolkit throughout this book. I'll break down each of these tools in more detail in the coming chapters. Of course, as with everything, having an expert walk you through these tools to apply to your exact situation is by far the best. However, I will do my best to break down these tools so that you can start using them today and see results immediately.

# The Clean Slate Method

As I stated before, the Clean Slate Method is part of the Triad of Connection. This is a method we adapted from T.W. Jackson and is your first stop in the Triad of Connection. As stated in the previous chapter, The Clean Slate Method allows you to wipe the past clean.

The reason we start here is because in so many marriages, the same problems from the past keep coming up over and over again. In traditional therapy, a marriage counselor will have you keep bringing up past discretions and upsets with the idea that somehow bringing them up all the time will make things better. I don't know about you, but for me, this made my marriage worse, not better. We've also found this to be the case with thousands of other married businessmen we've worked with.

Bringing up the past is like driving a high-performance sports car. This sports car happens to be your marriage. And bringing up the past is like driving this high-performance machine speeding down the highway of life while looking in the rearview mirror to try to move forward.

When you're looking backward the entire time, trying to drive forward to get where you want to go, you will inevitably crash. And to top it off, each time you crash, that's another negative experience, another negative feeling, tipping the scales further out of your favor.

These consistent negative feelings and experiences become something that gets brought up in marriage counseling. It's almost as if the therapy causes fights that then get to be discussed in therapy. One fuels the other in what ends up being a continuous, perpetual cycle. It just doesn't work.

So what we need to do is wipe the slate clean, draw a line in the sand, and say we are starting from this point. Our marriage and our relationship are starting from this new point going forward. The Clean Slate Method allows you to do this, thus, tipping the scales back to neutral. Now, the scales being at neutral is going to feel amazing because it's been so bad for so long. However, we won't stop there, so don't worry about that.

The essence here is taking true and unequivocal accountability. "I have wronged you. This is how I have let you and me down by behaving in this way." Accountability preceding an apology is a very powerful combination and not something most men consider, let alone know how to do or are willing to do.

Have you ever apologized to your wife only to have it backfire?

An apology is like a scalpel. A scalpel, if used correctly, can save lives and can cut away years of damage, but if used incorrectly, it can swiftly sever the heart from the body permanently.

Millions, if not billions, of dollars have been paid in lawsuits that could have been saved with an effective apology.

For example, an Eddie Bauer store that wrongly accused a black teenager, Alonzo Jackson, of shoplifting a shirt he had purchased the day before had to pony up $85 million in a lawsuit. His dad said that an apology would have sufficed. Eddie Bauer did make a weak public apology. But they never apologized privately to Alonzo or his father.

However, when an apology is done correctly, it can truly perform what seems to be a miracle.

I am sure you have heard of many instances where not only women and men take partners back after affairs but also where families have forgiven murderers, rapists, and others who have done things much worse than most couples do to each other.

There is a "formula" for an effective apology.

In many instances, this "formula" has proven to be the "turnaround point" in healing a relationship.

This "formula" is called The Clean Slate Method because it has the power to "wipe the slate clean" so a relationship can begin to heal.

So, what's the purpose of an apology?

Ask most anyone the purpose of an apology, and they may tell you that it is to admit that you were wrong.

An admission of wrongdoing.

This definition makes sense because that is what most of us have been taught, either explicitly or implicitly.

And even the Oxford English Dictionary (OED) says "apology" means a defense, justification, or excuse.

And that is exactly the way most of us apologize... "I am sorry, but..."

And it is exactly why we are in so much hot water and pain in many of our relationships. And why we live the following nightmare again and again.

Here's an example:

Tom comes home late from work again, maybe even carrying a dozen roses.

"I am sorry I am late."

"Saying you're sorry ain't going to cut it," Carol sneers, "and the flowers aren't going to work either."

Tom, visibly upset now says,

"I said I WAS SORRY!"... "What else can I do...damn it?" (and you know how the rest goes)

Now, if Tom can't make an effective apology for being tardy, what are the odds he can apologize for bigger transgressions?

So, I want you to try and consider a different purpose for an apology. One that will be far more effective for you is taking responsibility for a rift in the relationship.

Let's replay the Tom and Carol scenario.

(Tom has been staying late at the office due to a big job he just landed. Tom is under pressure to complete a project that's behind schedule. He arrives home an hour late for the third time this month.)

Tom: (Walking in the door) Hey, Babe. I know I'm late. You must be so angry and frustrated waiting around for me.

Carol: I am frustrated and a little angry.

Tom: I understand, and I'd feel the same way in your shoes. I feel so under pressure at work, and I am letting that get in the way of our relationship. I promised you I would be home by six and keep letting you down. When people let me down like this, I feel like I'm not important, and I want you to know that's not the case--you are the most important thing in the world to me.

Carol: Well, I do know that there is a lot of stuff going on at the office.

Tom: I appreciate you understanding, and I want you to know that I feel so terrible for letting you down.

What is also really important is that Tom never says he was wrong for being late. He says how he feels and that he is responsible for the rift in the relationship.

See the difference.

So part of the power of The Clean Slate Method is to undo our past programming on the meaning of an apology and begin to accept the "new" purpose of taking responsibility for the rift in the relationship.

## How To Go From "Bad" To "Worse"

Before we get into the "what to say," here are some old apology habits and mistakes you do not want to make. You will take your problems from bad to worse at 70 MPH if you make the following mistakes:

Too much emphasis on who's right and who's wrong. Remember our new definition. Accept responsibility for the rift. Are you trying to save face? Or save your relationship? Also, remember the saying, "Would you rather be right or happy?"

Insincerity (just trying to placate). This is a knee-jerk response that is hazardous to our relationships. Do not fire off volleys of "I'm sorry, but...". This only adds fuel to the fire. Also, your attitude is everything. We can tell when someone is being sincere or not. Get into her world. How do you think she feels? If you felt that way, regardless of the circumstances, how would you want someone to speak to you when you believe they made you feel this way?

Expecting and even demanding complete forgiveness. This is so big; we will talk about it some more later.

Expecting the other party to admit their wrongdoing. When using The Clean Slate Method, the other person will often admit to "wrongdoing"...but you cannot expect this. You are simply taking ownership of your side of the relationship without expecting them to do the same. This is a very common pitfall most men fall into and will set you back big time.

Remember, YOU HAVE TO TAKE RESPONSIBILITY FOR THE RIFT.

That means if your partner had an affair, you have to take responsibility. Very often, they will take their share too. But once again, it is a mistake, and The Clean Slate Method will not work if you expect and/or demand them to take responsibility for their share.

Apologizing too soon. The bigger the transgression, the longer you should wait to apologize. It would seem insincere and placating to offer an apology minutes after your affair is discovered. Make sense?

## The Method Itself

We're going to start with a Clean Slate Letter. Why a letter? Because it will allow you the time and space to put your thoughts and feelings down on paper without allowing yourself to stumble or get triggered. As men, communicating our feelings can be very foreign to us; thus, it doesn't always come out the way we intend.

Even worse, when we communicate our feelings, we open ourselves up to get hurt, and that's when our harshest defense mechanisms can take over - lashing out, yelling, stonewalling, or simply walking out. None of these gets us the result we're after, so we start with a letter.

Also of note, this letter is your chance to come clean about all the problems in your marriage. Your wife already knows all of this, and it won't come as a surprise to her. What will probably come as a surprise is you admitting them.

Now you're only going to write this from your perspective, the things you have done wrong, the indiscretions that have happened. This is not a place to bring up anything your wife has done or any grievances you've had or still have with her. You are taking radical and complete ownership of your side. The Clean Slate Letter is also not the place for you to share with her a big indiscretion, such as an affair or drug habit, that she doesn't know about. You are simply coming from a place where you're letting her know that you're aware of your actions and how your actions may have affected her.

Do not drop a bomb in her lap with this letter. I repeat, do not do it.

You are simply coming from a place where you're letting her know that you're aware of your actions and how your actions may have affected her.

## Step 1

Your mindset is the most important aspect of this process. If you have the right mindset, your words will go a long way to working themselves out.

Before writing this letter, ensure you are sober in both body and mind. Of course, this means that you should not be writing this while sipping on your favorite bourbon. Tempting, I know, but please don't do this. I've coached many men back from the ledge who thought it would be a good idea to have a few drinks to calm their nerves and open themselves up, only to find they didn't get the result they were looking for...in fact, it was much worse. Write like you drive--sober.

Also, make sure you're in a good space mentally. You don't want to sit down and write this letter after a big fight or a long day. If you're feeling mentally defeated or tired, wait another day. Of course, don't use this as a perpetual excuse to not write the darn thing, but also be conscious of when you write it. If you're usually tired after a long day at the office, write the letter in the morning or at lunch. If you had a fight with your wife or someone else, for that matter, then wait until you've calmed down before sitting down to write your "clean slate letter."

This letter is pivotal in turning your marriage around, so you want to treat it with as much respect as you do your marriage. In The Activation Method course, a coach will often review and help a man rewrite his letter three to four times before he delivers it. I can't do that for you in this book, so I'm again going to emphasize the importance of ensuring you're in a good headspace before you write this letter.

Also, make sure you write the letter in a place where you feel comfortable and where you won't be disturbed. A coffee shop is OK. If you can, find a place where you won't be bothered, and you can

THE CLEAN SLATE METHOD

focus on the task at hand. I recommend noise-canceling headphones and turning your chair to face a wall, so you don't get distracted when you're writing if you plan on writing this letter outside of your own home.

If you are already in The Activation Method, please lean on your coach. Your coach is a professional who has helped thousands of men like you write their letters and deliver them in a way that helps get the intended result. He can also help you if the result doesn't pan out the way we want it to the first time.

## Step 2

Acknowledge how your wife feels! This means you must take time to put yourself in her shoes. Seriously. Imagine what she might be going through, feeling the way she feels.

You really want to understand what's occurring for her. And this is where you want to think about what it would be like to be her in a relationship with you. Most women report feeling alone, scared, and frustrated that their husband hasn't stepped to the line. I don't blame them, do you?

Your wife was "sold" a dream of who you would become and the things you would do. Did that turn out the way she imagined it would be? The way she hoped it would be? If the answer is no, take responsibility for your part and imagine what she must be feeling.

I know, she's at fault here too, and it isn't as bad as she makes it out to be… I've heard it all a thousand times. Forget that story and get into her world because, to her, the way she feels is very real, and if you can't get past your own ego, then this will never work. It isn't all your fault, but you get to own your part. For this letter to work, you have to only take into account your actions and how those actions, or words, made the other person feel.

Example: Let's say you and your wife have grown apart. For whatever reason, you're not having sex often, and your relationship seems more like the two of you are roommates that only talk about the logistics of the kids and life rather than having passionate sex and conversations. In this case, you can imagine what it would feel like for a woman to be in this sort of relationship. The first thing that comes to my mind is, "man, that must feel awfully lonely and depressing. I can't imagine any woman feeling good about being in a short-term relationship, let alone a long-term one, where she doesn't feel a connection." To most women, connection is like oxygen--without it, they die. If you don't have a deep connection with your wife, then she feels as if she's dying. Get it?

As another example, you may say, you may come to the realization that you haven't stepped up to be the leader in your family and that you've fallen into the trap of being passive, which forced her to take on the Alpha role in the relationship. You may say that it wasn't your intention to leave her by herself and that you'd imagine she must be lonely in that state.

So again, for example, if you're admitting that you've been in DEER mode: Defending, Excusing, Explaining, Reacting, then you write something like this:

I realized that over the last few years, I have been reacting and losing my cool when we get into a disagreement, which has only pushed us further apart. That's never been my intention. I imagine being in a relationship where you're constantly arguing would be unfulfilling, and you didn't sign up for this. I haven't stepped up in our marriage to be the man, the leader, and the husband you've always wanted me to be.

Get into her world without judgment.

I often coach men to think of their wives' stories or, said another way, the way their wife might feel about her relationship with you as if she was a close friend of yours. How would you empathize with her in that situation?

Be careful not to say, "I know how you feel." This will likely offend her right away, and it doesn't really acknowledge her feelings in any way. What you want to say is: I'd imagine that you must feel so_____and_____...

Nobody will ever be mad when you are exploring how they feel.

Many times they will try and help you. In fact, if a person is mad and you say: You must be so angry...

They may say: Well, I wouldn't say angry...maybe just a little upset...

Or...

They may say: I am beyond angry...I am hurt...

Either way, you both come out ahead because you have a better understanding of their feelings, and they feel heard and acknowledged.

Since you are writing this in a letter, you won't get that instant feedback, and thus it's very important that you come across as being empathetic and taking ownership of what I call "your side of the street."

## Your Side of the Street

If you've heard me speak publicly or online, you might have heard me use this analogy. Either way, I'm going to share it with you here.

Imagine that you live in a suburban tract home, and you walk out of your house only to see your neighbor's house across the street. You immediately start to criticize your neighbor for his grass not being cut and the trash cans still in the street, even though collection day was two days ago.

As you turn around, after your tirade in the middle of the street, you look at your house--the grass is also unkept, trash on the lawn, and you see a house in need of a new paint job.

Instead of complaining about your neighbor's house, fix yours.

Take ownership of your side of the street before pointing fingers at anyone else. Simple as that.

By the way, in my over two decades of coaching experience, I've never met anyone with a "perfect house," so you might as well just stop criticizing others… especially those you claim to love (like your wife).

## Step 3

The Why. This is usually first and foremost on their mind. For example, if you were late to a big event, or if you made a promise you didn't keep, or if you had an affair...

She wants to know why?

This is very dangerous ground if you are not in the right mindset, as we discussed. You have to take responsibility for the rift! Let me say that again, you have to take responsibility for the rift.

You do this by examining your feelings or behaviors responsible for the rift.

Let's take a really tough scenario.

Let's say Carol has an affair, and Tom is the one who wants to heal the relationship.

Okay? It was Carol, not Tom, that had the affair. But Tom is taking responsibility for the rift.

So what is the feeling and/or behavior that Tom had that caused the rift? The rift that contributed to the affair.

So Tom may say: You must have felt (feel) so alone and unloved. I felt so insecure about our financial future and unsure of my ability as a provider that I put work before our relationship, us, and our family. I left you alone to fend for yourself emotionally. When things started to drift between us, I wasn't sure how to fix them, so I thought if I turned to work and made more money, things would work themselves out. I now see how doing that only created more disconnect between us.

What may happen at this point is that Carol may burst into tears (and Tom, too, if he's in the room while arol is reading the letter) because this is the first time she has felt heard and/or acknowledged. This may be the start of catharsis and healing of the relationship.

No matter what happens, Tom needs to continue to step 4.

## Step 4

Let them know you were affected too.

IMPORTANT: Do not use this as an opportunity to tell them what they did, but rather by what you are taking responsibility for. From the example above:

Tom might say: I feel so much pain and feel so guilty that I was responsible for you feeling all alone. I feel so lonely now too. My insecurity has caused the loss of my best friend, my lover, and my wife.

## Step 5

Offer your apology without defense. What does that mean? To apologize, expecting nothing in return. Realize that your apology may not be enough for her and that you are vulnerable. What happens is totally up to them, and that's okay. Accept that they may not forgive you now or in the future.

This is the most powerful step of them all. It is the step that has the power to truly wipe the slate clean. But you can't expect it. Does that make sense?

Continuing with our example:

Tom may say: Carol, I know there are no words that can make up for the loneliness I caused. While I pray for your forgiveness, I do not and cannot expect it. I am truly sorry.

This is a place to simply come clean about what's gone on in the past. And what if any harm it's caused her. If she's bringing up complaints. Chances are she's hurt in one way or another. This is your chance to have what Jocko Willink calls Extreme Ownership. Nowhere in this letter should you blame her for anything. Nowhere in this letter should you blame anybody else except for your actions.

This is where you take, as the man, as the leader, as the wolf, complete ownership of everything that's transpired. Yes, I understand that there's been other wrongdoings and other things that have happened in your marriage. Yes, I get that your wife isn't perfect, and she's caused problems too. But this isn't the place to air that laundry.

This is simply the place for you to wipe the slate clean about your side of the street. We don't want to point fingers at your wife or anybody else for any of the wrongdoings or indiscretions that have happened. This is your shot at wiping the slate clean of all the things you've done. And this is important because you're the leader. And even if your ego jumps in and says to yourself that it's not your fault, she should apologize first or whatever their story comes up. This is not the place for that.

This is a place for you to be the man, for you to be the leader, and lead by example. We all know that leading by example is the most powerful way to lead. So that's what the Clean Slate letter gives you the ability to do. It allows you to be the first person to apologize or the first person to clear the air around anything that may be an issue in your marriage. This is your shot. To draw a line in the sand and say Hey, I recognize all these things in the past that were indiscretions that I did wrong, and I'm not going to do them again. And during the Clean Slate letter, you also want to write what you want.

So again, going back to a very common example of a man going into DEER mode and withdrawing from the relationship, the wife has had to step up and be the Alpha.

A man might say:

I realized that over the last few years, I've taken a backseat in the marriage and counted on you to raise the kids and make decisions. I imagine it would be both frustrating and lonely, feeling like you are all alone in this relationship. It both angers and saddens me that it got to this point. I only wish that I knew then what I know now. I want you to be able to be the feminine goddess I see inside of you and to work with you on our relationship. I want to take the reins in our marriage, not to be controlling, but to give you a break so that you can fully express all sides of yourself, knowing you have a man that will catch you should you ever fall. Now that I understand where I lost myself, I can now clearly see a path back to the man we both knew was inside me. I want to be that man for you but also for me.

## Step 6

State what you want. This is a very powerful step as you get the chance to start to take the reins of leadership back in your marriage. By declaring what you want, you set the direction, or vision, for where your marriage could go.

As with anything powerful, it needs to be wielded properly, so it doesn't backfire.

Continuing with the example, Tom might say in his letter: What I want is for both of us to feel connected and know that we're in this together. I want you to feel that you can come to me with anything; no matter what it is, I'll hold space for you and listen. I want us to get to know each other, not the old versions of ourselves, but the current versions of ourselves. I also want us to have more fun together as a loving couple.

## Step 7

Delivery. Now that you have written your letter, it's time to deliver it. As with the start of these steps, it's important that you deliver it at a time when both you and your wife will be sober. You don't want to deliver it when you've been drinking, after a long day, or after a fight.

If you and your wife are no longer living together and she has stopped all contact, you can mail her the letter or give it to a trusted friend. Of course, make sure you don't violate any court orders that may be in place.

When you hand them the letter, do so with love in your heart and eyes. Tell them that you put some of your feelings down on paper and would greatly appreciate it if they could take some time to read the letter without expectations.

You may choose to stay in the room, but I often coach the men to leave their wives alone so they can absorb the letter without any reaction.

I have seen countless men, even after divorce, turn their marriages around with the steps outlined in this book. It all starts with this step of the process.

It is our small transgressions that build up day after day that can really erode our relationships with our friends, coworkers, bosses, children, and lovers.

This gradual erosion finally gives way to a full-blown landslide that needs serious repair. Try to remember the adage that an ounce of prevention is worth a pound of cure.

I would highly suggest that you commit The Clean Slate Method to memory. But, even for those who can store data like a camel stores water, many times in the heat of the moment, we can't recall the right words.

This is where understanding the mindset, focusing on the relationship, and not being right or wrong will save you.

Coming from the right place in your heart will get your relationship back on track faster than carefully crafted words.

Use common sense. If she just found out that you killed her favorite pet, you probably don't want to apologize right away.

The bigger the mistake/transgression, the longer you should wait to apologize.

This is just a simple example of how the Clean Slate Method can be utilized. If you'd like training on the Clean Slate method and how to read through it, go to www.thepowerfulman.com/book to get a copy of the Clean Slate Method and see examples of how it's worked for other men like you.

**Let's review the steps of The Clean Slate Letter:**

Step 1: You are going to sit down and write a letter listing out your shortcomings during the entirety of your marriage in more of a story format rather than bullet points. Remember, this has nothing to do with anything that she has done. You cannot use this letter to blame her. Use the conversational tone above as a reference.

Step 2: Tell her what you want in our relationship and how you want to show up. Tell her what your plan is. Here's an example:

[all the things that have happened]... and what I want is for us to be a team. I want you to feel loved and appreciated every single day. I want you to know in your heart of hearts that I am your man and that I will always be here for you. I'm going to continue this journey of working on myself and diving deeper into what it means to be a powerful husband, a powerful father, and a powerful man. And if I stumble, I promise you that I will get right back up and keep marching forward with you along my side. You mean the world to me, and I now understand a little more how to show it to you.

Step 3: Make sure you actually handwrite this letter. A handwritten letter carries more weight than one typed up.

Step 4: Reread your letter and make sure there isn't any "sting" left in the letter and it's from a place of engaged indifference and love.

Step 5: Tell your wife you love her and that you took the time to write her a letter. Give her the letter, and then you can leave. Do not expect a reaction. You are not writing this letter to "get" anything from her. This is you wiping the slate clean. Do not expect her to do the same. She will be able to tell if there are unsaid expectations. When you do this, you turn the letter into a transaction, not an act of love.

Step 6: Relax. You've done what you can here.

Of course, every circumstance is different, and in an ideal world, you would have a coach trained in this to help you with your letter. We're human, and as such, we're emotional creatures who sometimes put our feet in our mouths or say the wrong thing. In this case, you may intend to say something sweet, but it might come off as harsh to the reader. Short of having that coaching, just do the best you can. Imperfect action is better than perfect inaction.

It's common for the wife to get upset and lash out or stonewall (close down) when she receives this letter. If this is the case, she might be upset that you are doing this now after all this time. "Where was this a year ago?" She might be thinking to herself. Whatever her reaction, remember--engaged indifference. It's her experience, not yours.

Here are some common mistakes men make when delivering their Clean Slate Letters:

1. Men wait to deliver the letter when their wife has been drinking. This is not the time. Alcohol can make us more emotional and cause us to react in ways we regret. Also, you should not be under the influence of alcohol or drugs.

2. Men casually throw their wives a letter as if it's something their wife has to do, and they don't care if she reads it or not. She'll find this demeaning and lacking in effort. When this happens,

some women simply file the letter in the trash or a drawer and never read it.

3. Do not give it to her when you are upset. You are not practicing engaged indifference if you are upset; therefore, you need to wait until you're calm and ready.

4. Do not give this to her when she's upset. This will most likely make her feel that you're doing this to get on her good side, and although you might be, don't use this powerful tool in that manner.

5. If you aren't talking to each other and she's moved out, mail it to her. I recommend certified mail where she has to sign for it.

6. DO NOT BLAME HER. I know I'm repeating this, but I can't tell you how many times our coaches have to help a guy who thinks he's written the perfect Clean Slate Letter edit his letter multiple times before it's good to go out.

7. Don't overpromise. If you've been lying to her about the ways in which you are going to change, then call them out and be realistic about the changes you'll be making. She may have heard it all before, so don't sugarcoat it. Tell her the truth. Here's an example: I realize that I've made a lot of promises in the past, so I'm hesitant to do so here in this letter. I'd imagine that if I were you, I'd be expecting to be disappointed by any promise that came out of my mouth. That pains me deeply to think that I've violated your trust. What I will tell you is that I'm investing in getting expert help and accountability to ensure that this time I'm able to follow through on the one commitment that is the most important to me - that's gaining your trust back. I am not asking for anything from you. I just

want you to know that I love you, and I hope that you see the changes I'm making are positive and lasting.

8. Delivering the letter too soon.. Rushing it before she has had a chance to see some real change.

Remember, actions speak louder than words. We've all heard that, and we've all witnessed it in our own lives. It's now time for you to showcase the wolf inside of you. Be wise, open, loving, and fierce. Let those around you see that your eyes are open, and let your actions speak for themselves.

The Clean Slate Letter is also not a "one and done," but rather the beginning of several important, structured conversations that must follow its delivery. Think of it as a beginning rather than an end. The specifics of when and how to have these conversations is best supported and facilitated by an experienced coach who can walk you through the process specific to your situation.

I can't emphasize the importance of getting help with your letter enough. If you can't invest in getting a professional to walk you through this process, then please at least have a few trusted advisors take a look. Your marriage is not to be taken lightly, and when you consider the financial cost of divorce, let alone its emotional toll, I think you'll find the investment well worth it.

If you'd like to see some examples of Clean Slate Letters and reactions from wives, go over to www.thepowerfulman.com/book

When our friend Dave delivered his Clean Slate Letter, he was nervous. Things around the house had gotten a little better, and when things have been as bad at home for as long as they had for Dave, it's easy to get nervous about upsetting your wife and going back to the way they had been, but Dave was encouraged by his couch to set the scene and follow through.

Dave waited for an evening when the kids would be away and he and his wife would have some time together. He made sure that his wife had time to unwind and relax before he approached her. Dave's coach advised him to hand it to her in person and explain the intent of the letter.

As Dave sat down on the couch next to his wife with his letter neatly folded into the envelope he held in his hand, his wife could tell something was up. She naturally looked at Dave with a bit of suspicion as she sat up to face him.

Dave's coach had prepared him for this, and Dave handled it like a master.

Dave took a deep breath, looked his wife in the eyes, and began to tell her how much he loved her and how, although things had been tough over the last few years, he still loved her very deeply. Dave told her he had written a letter to her and asked if she would read it to herself as he sat beside her. She agreed.

As Dave's wife read the letter, tears began to fall down her face. She looked at Dave lovingly, and now, Dave, with tears in his eyes, waited to hear what she thought.

Dave's wife leaned over and gave him a deep hug and said, "Dave, this is what I've been waiting for. Thank you for being courageous enough to do the work. I love you so much!"

Dave and his wife continued to embrace each other and then spent the rest of the evening talking, similar to the way they had when they first met--connected and free.

# The Hidden Motives Technique

The second part of the Triad Connection is something that we call The Hidden Motives Technique. The Hidden Motives Technique has been specifically designed to allow your wife to be seen and heard. Women have often told us that they want to be seen and heard and desired to have a fulfilling relationship with their husbands.

The Hidden Motives Technique gives you two of those three deep desires a woman has, and often, we hear from the women who are recipients of this technique that they feel, for the first time in their marriage, really gotten by their husband as if their husband really understands them for the first time. And as you can imagine, this is an amazing feeling for anybody but especially for a woman.

The Hidden Motives Technique doesn't require your wife to know anything you're doing. Hence the name "Hidden Motives Technique.". What you're going to do is validate your wife.

We all know there's this cliche that when women share with their husbands, their husbands rush to solve the problems and the women get upset. You see, your wife doesn't want you to solve her problems. She just wants you to listen. More often than not, when that's when we as men go to solve the problems of our partners, it causes more strife in the marriage.

So, rather than bringing you and your wife closer, it pushes you apart. This can be really hard for most guys because the problems that wives bring to us seem so obvious and easily solvable. However, that is not her intent. Her intent is simply to empty her berries and share with you what is going on. We'll talk more about emptying her basket in a bit.

Emptying the berries is an analogy that we use at The Powerful Man and comes from the idea that in prehistoric times, men would go off on a hunt together and, when going on a hunt, to kill the woolly mammoth to bring back the food to the tribe, to your family. A man would have to be extremely quiet to not scare the prey. The man would have to sneak up on the prey and only do sign language to other fellow men, maybe a quick grunt or small call, so they could get close enough to the prey to kill them, clean them, and bring them back home.

On the other hand, women would be the gatherers in the tribe, and they would go out to pick berries. But when a woman went out to pick berries, she would go with other women to make sure that she was safe.

Men are naturally stronger than women. So when a woman is out, she needs to be with other women to protect her from other warring tribes who want to kidnap and rape her as well as the saber tooth tiger down by the bushes. And so, during these outings, women would talk to each other.

Instead of being quiet, they had to share knowledge openly. For example, they would explain to each other that, hey, you want to get the berries, but go get the berries on the right side of the river, not the left side of the river, because the berries on the right side of the river are fresh and the berries the left side of the river are poisonous but don't get the dark purple berries. Get the red berries and watch out for the big tree near the bank, because inside of it lives a giant snake. And as the women were talking they were also scaring off predators. And this is one reason women became so much more verbose than men, often talking a lot about what's going on throughout their day.

As a husband, you get the opportunity of emptying your wife's berry basket so she can start fresh. Otherwise, she's carrying around this burden. When you're emptying her berries, it simply allows her at the end of the day to download how her day went.

She might start to explain to you how her day was and instead of ignoring her or zoning off, you want to get into her day, and when she complains, you want to use The Hidden Motives Technique.

One of the biggest problems I used to struggle with was knowing how to meet my partner's needs without her having to tell me what they were.

This caused major problems in the relationship.

I'd go to work every day and do my best to slay the dragon and bring home a prize worth celebrating.

But, no matter what I did, it never seemed to land.

I remember one time, I'd just landed a six-figure contract (back then, it was my biggest deal to date), and I'd gone above and beyond to get it.

Late nights, awkward negotiations, coming up with creative ways to handle every objection, and even wining and dining the client a few times.

I knew there was no point in sharing with my wife what might happen, so I waited until the deal was done before I walked through the door with a bunch of red roses, a bottle of champagne, and a big "Baby, I did it!"

Finally, that day arrived.

I'd played it over in my mind so many times, how it would go...

She'd call me during the day, I'd play cool, not mention anything to her, just drop in a little "Oh, I've got something you might like, I'll tell you tonight when I see you..." just to pique her curiosity.

I'd finish early, stop by the flower shop to pick up some roses (her favorite), buy a bottle of our favorite champagne, walk through the door, put them onto the kitchen island, walk upstairs, go over to her, share my win and she'd instantly be all over me.

This meant we could buy that dream house we'd been looking at, go on that vacation, and replenish our savings. Basically, it was the key to our kingdom (for the most part).

Well, it didn't go like that.

Instead of walking in and being admired for slaying the dragon and bringing home a feast that would feed us for months, I was scorned like a pauper who stole bread out of the trash bins.

I walked through the door, roses, and champagne in hand, and before I shared my victory, she said:

"Why didn't you take the trash out?"

WTF! Are you serious!?

Couldn't she see that I'd finished early, I had her favorite roses, our favorite champagne, and I'd piqued her curiosity earlier that day--had she forgotten already?

At that point, I LOST IT!

What I didn't realize at the time was that despite my big win, my wife's love tank was running dry while I was working.

She was fed up with me letting her make decisions on what we should eat for dinner.

She was fed up with reminding me to take the trash out.

She was tired of the times when I'd cut her down or ignore her when she'd try to tell me about her day because I was burned out from the business.

And she was sick and tired of telling me what she needed because I'd too often say those fatal words all of us men say: "Just tell me what you need, and I'll do it." The reality is that no woman wants to have to tell her man what to do to make her happy. If she does, then he becomes another thing she's gotta manage in her life.

That isn't sexy, and that doesn't enable her to relax into her most sensual side, the side where you get the least amount of arguments, the most amount of admiration, and plenty of great sex.

You see, women can be like Rubik's Cubes. You can spend hours trying to figure out the right combination just to get nowhere, but when you learn how to play the game right, you can crack the code within minutes.

This is what The Hidden Motives Technique does.

It enables you to have drama-free communication that leads to a passionate, loving, and peaceful relationship.

Essentially, it shows you how to meet your wife's needs without her having to tell you what they are (and without having to be telepathic).

Now, you might be thinking...

"My wife's different; you've never met her. How can you tell me how to meet her needs? I've been married to her for ten years, and I still can't do it. How are you going to be able to?"

That's a fair point, and to be honest, women are all different. But just like baking a cake, they all have some of the same basic ingredients.

When you add these into the recipe, at the right time and in the right order, the cake rises regardless of whether you're baking a birthday cake or a red velvet cake.

So, let's dive in.

## Step 1

Take her berries out of the basket!

I'm going to cut to the chase here--women MUST unload. A woman that isn't able to unload becomes irritable, kinda like a volcano ready to erupt. Who do you think she erupts onto?

Yep, you, and just like molten lava, when she does erupt, it burns!

What do I mean by unload?

Again, let's go back in time to the days when we were cavemen. You had hunters and gatherers. Men were hunters; we would go out from the cave hunting the big prey. And when you're hunting the big prey, you can't talk to be stealthy, right? You make grunts, hand gestures here and there, and point where each other has to go. But if you make noises, the prey is going to get away, and that means no food for your family.

So as men, anthropologically, we've been conditioned and hardwired in our brains to talk in very short bursts.

You ask a guy, hey, how's your day?

What does he say?

"Good," right?

Now, women are different.

While the men are out hunting, the women are gonna go out and gather and they're going to go with other women.

It's really important for them to constantly communicate because if they're going to go pick berries (for example), they need to know: What berries are in season? Where are the berries located? Are the berries located by the river? Which are the poisonous berries, and which ones are safe to eat? Where are the ripe berries this time of year? Etc.

For the woman, if she comes back in with the wrong berry, it could be poisonous, and she could kill her whole tribe or whole family, so when she asks another woman where to look for the berries, she'd probably hear back something like this:

"Get the red berries by the big tree that sits on the ridge around the bend with the small leaves that's next to the small bush. It's right next to the river, over there with the big rock. But don't pick the berries near the oak tree because a plant that looks similar near that tree will cause intense stomach pain."

It's all very descriptive. Also, when the woman is out there, she has to be in constant communication because she wants to be aware of the Sabretooth tiger that might be around because, typically, she isn't as strong as men.

Think about what happens when you ask a woman how her day was. If you ask a guy, you'll most likely get a few words here and there, but if you ask a woman, she's gonna give you a breakdown!

"Well, today was so interesting because Janine, you know how Janine is; Janine is married to Jake. Well, Jake. Jake, you know Jake, Jake's a plumber. He works with Rick, and Rick's a really interesting guy too. And, you know, when he goes out there, he works at Sears. But then Janine, you know, we'll go through, and she was really ratty about this. But then I stopped by the café; I got a coffee, but not the hot coffee. I got one of those cold coffees with espresso."

She'll go on and on before she comes back to the point of what her day was

like, right?

This is what's called "a meadow" or, giving a meadow description. It's as if she's walking through the meadow describing her surroundings to ensure you don't eat the wrong berries.

And so, at the end of the day, she's gathered all of these berries throughout her whole day, which is a heavy basket for her. She comes back home to you, the man, and then what she needs to do is unload that basket. Unload those berries, unload her day, download it onto you, the man.

Now, as a strong man, your job is to collect those berries.

Just let her dump her basket into yours.

She's not looking for you to solve the problem, so don't offer solutions. I realize how tough this is, but it's critical that you only listen.

She's just looking to unload those berries and all that she's gathered throughout the day because if she doesn't, that provides stress and anxiety.

She's got to unload it so she can be in her femininity, and it's here where intimacy comes from.

## Step 2

Most relationships work with one person being more masculine and the other person being more feminine. This creates polarity and a spark, kind of like what happened when you first met your wife.

You've been on your own, going about your life being masculine; she's been doing the same and being feminine; you guys come together, and BAM!

The trouble is, over time, this gets lost, and with it, the polarity goes away, and so does the spark, often leading to less intimacy, desire, and sex.

I'm about to share one way you can get this back.

Your woman wants to be seen, heard, and desired. An easy way for you to do that through communication is validation, and really looking at her with empathy.

So, for example, in my marriage, we've decided that my wife takes care of the kids, and I work.

I may come home after a busy day and my wife might immediately greet me with, "The kids are going CRAZY!"

Now, the old Doug might have said something like:

"Oh, geez, I get it. My day was crazy, too. I had to redo some of our contracts. I had a negotiation that fell through, and I had to lay off one of our staff!"

In this place, she's not going to feel seen or heard because I'm missing the point.

Let's switch this around, same scenario, and we'll have Doug 2.0 using The Hidden Motives Technique.

So, for example, for Doug 2.0, in his marriage, they've decided that his wife takes care of the kids, and he works.

He may come home after a busy day, and his wife might immediately greet him with, "The kids are going CRAZY!"

He says, "Oh, wow, I'd imagine that would be frustrating, and it'd be really draining."

What he's doing is getting into her world without fixing it. He's validating what she's telling him, and then empathizing with her.

This allows her to take the berries out of her basket.

If Doug 2.0 wants to take this a step further, he could say: "Wow, that's really crazy. You know, I can imagine that being really tiring and really frustrating, going through that."

Once she responds, he may even say, "What else?", giving her permission to talk more and share more, and then she might say, "Oh, well, then my mother called and, you know, my mom's just not feeling well."

Doug 2.0 might respond with, "Oh, man. That's horrible. I hope she's okay. I'd imagine that puts a lot more anxiety on you, especially with the kids going crazy, right?"

In the house, Doug 2.0 has now created a space where his wife feels relaxed, almost like she's become putty.

Validation allows her to feel safe and comfortable, allowing her to feel seen by you, her man, and desired because you're giving her your time.

Not once do you go in there and try to fix it, not once do you say, "Oh, I know the greatest doctor. We need to get your mom an appointment." No, it's not what she's looking for.

You can do that later if you want to or if she specifically asks for your advice.

But at this point, it's for you to validate what's going on for her in her world without trying to dominate her with what's going on in your world.

By actually validating and going deep into her experience, you're going to be able to pull out much more information, she's going to feel seen and heard, and she'll look up to you with admiration again.

And if that's something that's been missing in your relationship, this is a great next step after the first one.

The next step is for you to start active listening. This looks like saying "Mmmmm hmmmm," while at the same time nodding your head and continuing to look at her, giving her your full attention.

This will bring you even closer together and make her feel as if she is the most important person in the world to you.

Often when women have emotional affairs or even sexual affairs, it's because they find a guy that is willing to hold that space for them and be that vessel she empties into.

By default, when she empties into that vessel, she feels safe in that space, which pulls her in, and she wants to be in it more--she feels more connected in that place.

We've seen this play out in the relationships of some men who join The Activation Method.

They didn't realize the disconnect they were creating in their relationship. Instead, they thought that they were doing all the right things by going out there and leaving everything on the battlefield of business but bringing home nothing to their wife and kids.

So when their wife tried to tell them how her day was, they didn't have the capacity to hold a space that she could empty into. Instead, they'd go to the fridge to crack a beer, pour a cocktail, or bury their head in their phone.

## Step 3 - Desire

Your woman needs to feel desired by you. It's a need.

Think about James Bond for a second. As a classical stereotype for a masculine male, what does he do? He showcases desire very covertly for the woman, and the woman responds by being very feminine. So how do you make your wife feel desired?

How do you communicate that desire? How do you show it?

Well, one of the ways you can do this is by utilizing your wife's love language and do it without asking her what her love language is!

Now, in case you don't know, the theory behind a love language is that we all show love differently. There are five that are typically talked about, and you can read more in Gary Chapman's book *The Five Love Languages: How to Express Heartfelt Commitment to Your Mate.*

1. Physical touch - hugging, kissing, holding hands

2. Quality time - spending time with one another where you're present

3. Acts of service - doing something for the other person

4. Gifts - buying something for the other person

5. Words of Affirmation - saying nice things

Let's look at your partner. Think back to the past--what did she do for you when you first got together?

Would she buy you a gift? Perhaps she would come over to your place with something she saw while out with her friends and thought of you.

Would she touch you physically, like put her hand on your back, rub your shoulders, or touch you often when she was smiling?

Did she want to spend quality time with you? This could look like sitting on the patio, being near one another, or perhaps even watching TV.

Did she help out around your place or help you with a project or something like that?

Or did she constantly tell you how amazing you are or compliment you?

Often, people do multiple things to show love, especially early in a relationship, so you want to look at what your wife does to show love for other people as well.

If you have kids, watch how she is around the kids, watch how she treats her mother, her father, and her friends.

Is she desiring to be in their physical presence? Or during holidays? Or for random reasons?

Is she always buying them gifts?

Or is she just a big hugger when she's around people?

Or is she always complimenting people?

Typically, the way that we showcase our love or desire for somebody is the way that we receive it.

It's your job as the man to observe your partner, see what she's doing in her natural environment, and then love her in how she gives it. This is how she's going to feel desired by you.

If your partner isn't seeing and feeling your love from you, then you're not speaking her language. It'd be like getting somebody who speaks Japanese and someone who speaks Russian in the same room and having them try to talk to each other.

They could be the greatest people in the world, but once they start talking, trying to connect, they're not going to understand each other, and they're gonna be missing what's being said.

However, if we get a translator in there or one happens to learn the other person's language, say it's the Russian, that starts speaking Japanese, all of a sudden, there's a conversation flow that's going on and an energetic exchange.

Using these techniques will allow your wife to feel connected to you regardless of how much time you're spending at work because the time you have together will be so special.

Just imagine for a moment that your wife's love language is gifts.

You're at the office, and in between meetings, you get some flowers delivered to her.

Or, if acts of service is her main language, then imagine you get home that evening, you walk through the door, ask her how her day was, you provide a space for her to unload, you then say, "Hey, I'm going to make dinner tonight, you relax," and pour her a glass of wine and place it next to the sofa.

What do you think will happen after or even during dinner?

Most likely, she's going to reach over to you, put her hand on yours, ask you how your day was, smile, and look at you like she used to. You guys will be together, and what happens next will be priceless.

Here's another example of The Hidden Motives Technique. You might come home late from work, and your wife's done with the kids, frustrated that they're not listening to her and feeling overwhelmed. As you get home, she might share this overwhelm with you and the fact that you're late and that she's having to take care of the kids without you. This is where you want to use The Hidden Motives Technique, and your response may go something like this….

"Wow. I'd imagine if I had to spend all day trying to wrangle a bunch of teenagers who weren't listening to me and disrespecting me, that would zap my energy, and if I thought my partner was off doing something fun, that would probably further infuriate me. I want you to know that I never want you to feel that way. I want you to always feel like you and I are in this together. And I want you to know that I was late simply because I was out closing another deal. And baby, I'm here for you. Let me take care of the kids."

The Hidden Motives Technique is really you getting into her world. Here's an example: "I'd imagine it'd be lonely being with little kids all day and not being able to have an adult conversation, that would drive me friggin crazy. I want you to be able to fully express yourself and be able to feel recharged at the end of each day. How can we do that together?"

These are easy examples of The Hidden Motives Technique. Below I'll share some other examples of how to use it. But the formula is fairly simple. When your wife has a grievance or complaint, and it's legitimate, not a shittest, but a legitimate complaint, what you want to do is say:

I imagine…

I suppose…

Wow, for me, this would be…

Essentially letting her know that you're stepping into her shoes, and then actually do it. What would it be like if you couldn't have an adult conversation that had kids running around all day? Every day? Sure, you can handle it. Sure. You could even do it for a week on end, but day after day, month after month, eventually, it would wear on you.

Oh, I imagined it would suck feeling lonely all day. And the truth is you don't want her to feel lonely so add that in. "I don't want you to feel lonely" and then tell her what it is you do want. "I want you to always know I'm here for you and that we're a team and a partnership." And that's the truth. You want her to know that, and this is where

The Hidden Motives Technique works so well. For a training on The Hidden Motives Technique and more information, go to www.thepowerfulman.com/book

Dave struggled at first using the Hidden Motives Technique. He would still catch himself going into DEER mode and at times he would forget the formula, but he could tell something was shifting. His wife started smiling more and it seemed as if she had been a withering plant that now was put into the sun and watered properly. She was blossoming once again.

His wife's response was enough for Dave to continue working on using the Hidden Motives Technique, and he not only used it with her, but also with his kids and co-workers.

Everyone started asking Dave what had changed. He seemed so much more engaged and happy. The truth was that Dave was allowing others to be seen and heard by Dave for the first time.

Dave worked with his coach to expand upon the ways in which he used this powerful technique. As he did so, it became easier and easier.

Dave was slipping into the WOLF and the people around him were loving him for it.

# The 5 Territories

At The Powerful Man, the introductory programs break life down into five territories. If you ever go through our programs, the territories can expand as they get more advanced. But for the beginning, I want you to think of your land and kingdom as broken up into five distinct territories. Those territories are self, health, wealth, relationships, and business.

Most married businessmen put all their focus into business because they've been sold a story that when you work hard, put your head down, make a lot of money for your family, buy the nice house, buy the guest house, go on all the trips, buy your wife jewelry and expensive cars, everybody's going to love you, and you're going to be happy. And when they wake up, usually around their mid-30s or 40s, they find out that that wasn't the case.

They look around, and the relationships have been severed. There's a lack of intimacy. At home, they've possibly lost connection with their children and don't have a lot of friends outside of the business. This is why at The Powerful Man, men fight to get their mojo back to save their marriage. To get unstuck and gain more clarity in life, they have to focus on the first territory, "self."

"Self" is all about taking care of you. When someone says that you're being selfish, really what they're saying is, hey, you're not doing what I want you to do. You're doing what you want to do. Therefore, you're being selfish. They make it sound like a bad thing. However, they're really saying, "I want to control you, and I want you to do what I want you to do when I want you to do it." Most men have become selfLESS rather than selfish.

In fact, for most guys, if I told them that they had a free day to do whatever they wanted, most men wouldn't know what to do with that time. Businessmen would go to work, often saying it's because they love it. But the truth is, they don't know what else to do.

Often, others don't have friends they could call to meet up with on a whim, to have a casual conversation, or do something fun. Can you remember the last time you did something fun just for yourself? Can't think of it? Most guys can't, either. Don't feel bad. The area of "self" is all about taking care of yourself. It's filling your cup.

All too often, as high achievers, we run around taking care of others, spilling into them.

Imagine holding a cup full of water up to your chest. The water represents your lifeforce. All day, you go around solving people's problems because it's easier for you than it is for them. You've got big shoulders and you can carry the burden. However, each time you put someone else ahead of yourself, you put a little water from your cup into theirs.

There's no problem with that. We're great men and we love helping people. I'm with you here.

However, at the end of the day, your cup is empty because you haven't filled it back up. You haven't filled yourself up with things you like to do and haven't recharged your batteries. Not only is this not self-serving, but when your cup is completely empty, you can become very needy and ask others to fill it.

When they don't, you resent them. You resent them for not automatically filling your cup when it's empty because you think they should.

This resentment leads to anger and frustration. In my experience, this comes out at the worst of times. You're already drained, stressed, and now your gas tank is empty.

You can see those people whose cups you've filled, but they aren't filling yours, so you explode or withdraw.

To your wife, this looks childish and even scary. I've had women tell me that there's nothing less sexy than a man who can't take care of himself and is needy. She doesn't want another child to take care of-- she wants a man.

This is why we tackle the area of "self" first. It may sound counterintuitive, but if you want to save your marriage, you must start here. This means finding things you love that make you feel whole and complete.

Finding time for you.

Finding time to do what you want to do. Think of this as dating yourself.

Take yourself out to lunch, take yourself out to dinner or a movie, treat yourself to a nice massage, or do something special just for you.

When's the last time you treated yourself like the king, like the alpha that you know you are?

If it's been a long time, then this is your chance. Although it could mean buying yourself that expensive watch or that nice car, it all too often has to do with how you treat yourself rather than what you buy yourself.

The second territory is the territory of "health."

As men age, our testosterone lowers, and we get busy. We're taking care of kids, and we get tired at the end of the day. All too often, we find ourselves cracking a beer or pouring a cocktail, snacking, sitting on the couch, and drowning out TV or something else that isn't good for our health. We begin to gain weight, and those few extra pounds quickly add up to 20, 30, or even more.

We become less energetic and less attractive, not only to our partners but also to ourselves. This lowers our self-confidence and leaves us a shell of the former man we used to be when we looked at ourselves in the mirror.

It's often said that men spend their entire lives building wealth, only to trade it all in for better health.

Now is your time to take care of your health. Yes, we still want to build wealth, but you also want to have fun now. Most men work hard, let their bodies go, and wait until retirement to do the things they want to do only to find that by that point their knees are bad, and they have to scoot around on an electric scooter to get around.

We want to move your health and fitness into what I call the "brush your teeth" category. My guess is that you brush your teeth everyday no matter what. In fact, you probably don't even think about it.

Men tend to have their fitness in the "get a massage" category where it happens only once in a blue moon. This has to change.

As men, we should get our blood tested for cholesterol, triglycerides, glucose, and other lipids and hormones such as testosterone, thyroid hormones, and cortisol. Additionally, modern DNA tests can provide insight into biological age and other genetic factors.

Also, if you're not going to the gym, start today. Hiring a trainer is the shortest and quickest way to close the gap. Hire a professional who can guide you along the journey and ensure you get there. This is also why coaching works. Sure, you might know how to lift weights, but are you doing it? If not, hiring a personal trainer or joining a class like CrossFit or something similar could hold you accountable until this becomes a familiar routine.

If weightlifting isn't your thing, try something different, like boxing, martial arts, or something else that will be rigorous. You will not only reap the rewards of pushing yourself outside of your comfort zone, but you will also increase your testosterone and human growth hormone by overcoming that resistance. As much as I like yoga, I won't do it alone.

This is also the time for a reality check on your diet. Keep a food log for the next five days, and be honest: Are you snacking on the kids' potato chips? Are you eating unhealthy crap that you know isn't good for you, yet you keep putting it in your body? How many cocktails are you having a night? How's your weekend binging going? What is your body fat level?

Changing your diet, for most men, is the start of changing your aesthetic appearance. It's always been said in the fitness industry that abs are made in the kitchen, not the gym. So start tracking your food and using a food tracking app like My Fitness Pal or many others to see where you're at and keep yourself in check so you can be the healthiest and sexiest version of yourself. This will make you feel better and increase your SMV, or sexual market value. The worst-case scenario here is that you end up being the sexy god you've always known yourself to be.

The third territory is "wealth."

Wealth is more about abundance than just about money. It's abundance in all areas of your life - spiritual abundance, financial abundance, and abundance with time.

Take some time to journal about the questions below.

What does "wealth abundance" mean to you?

What are you taking home after taxes?

Is that enough money to sustain your "hell yes lifestyle?"

If not, you get to take steps to make that a reality today.

What about time? Are you constantly complaining that you don't have enough time?

Hey, I've got news for you. We all have exactly the same amount of time, yet some of us tend to manage it much better than others. Why is that? Well, a lot of that is mindset. Yes, there are skills and tricks and time management techniques that help, but in my experience of over two decades of coaching, most of this has to do with your mindset.

And what about your spirituality? I'm not here to convert you to any particular religious dogma. If you're a Christian, then what's your relationship with Christ? If you're Jewish, are you going to the Temple? Buddhist, Muslim, or atheist? How is your spiritual practice serving you? For some of you, the religion you were brought up in hinders you, and it's time for a deep look and a possible change. For others, you've left your religion for one reason or another, and it's been calling you back.

The key here is to find out what serves you to your highest level.

What about meditation?

Almost all religions and spiritual practices have some form of meditation involved. It could be prayer, could be walking meditation, or it could be the traditional transcendental type of meditation. There are literally thousands of types of meditation available. The key is spending time in solitude to quiet your mind and connect with source or God, or whatever it is that you call your higher power. If you don't have a regular practice, then you're missing out.

Some of the most successful businesspeople in the world, from Steve Jobs to Ray Dalio, claim that meditation was the key to their success. As they say, success leaves clues.

The fourth territory is "relationships." The territory of "relationships" seems pretty obvious. But let's take inventory.

On a scale of one to 10. How would you rate your marriage?

Clearly, if you're reading this book, it's not a 10.

What about your relationship with your kids? With your parents? What about your siblings and coworkers? What about with your friends?

How would you rate those relationships? What would bring you one notch up--one notch higher?

Yes, you're reading this book. You're on your way to getting a better marriage and relationship with the people around you, and I applaud you. What else could you be doing? Are there courses that focus on this particular subject that's lacking for you? If so, sign up today.

Whenever I have the chance to sit down and speak with someone in their later years, I often ask them what was most important when they look back upon their life. One hundred percent of the time, either their proudest moments or their deepest regrets are around their relationships.

When was the last time you heavily invested in what I call "regret insurance" and did a deep dive into learning how to improve your relationships? In my experience, it's the best investment you can make.

The last territory is "business."

I've spent my whole career coaching and mentoring business owners and top-performing CEOs and executives, for whom business is usually the easiest territory to conquer. The businesses they run are usually not as successful as they could be because the psychology of the owner, the CEO, or the executives running the company aren't at the level they need to be. It's their mindset that becomes the limiting factor to their growth. Sure, tactics and tricks always help, but they're rarely the linchpin or big lever that will move the needle.

What moves the needle for a business is usually the leader's mindset, and when your marriage is in the crapper, often it's all you can think about at work. I know for me, when I was going through tough times in my marriage, the problems and the fights were all consuming. I couldn't focus and at times, it cost me dearly.

Similarly, when a marriage is working well, it provides the businessman with a stable space from which he can take off and soar. At The Powerful Man, we have companies that realize the ROI of having strong leaders with strong relationships, so they invest in their team and send them through our flagship program, The Activation Method. It's an investment into their best resource--their people.

As we look at these five territories, I want you to rate yourself overall on a scale of one to 10:

Where are you in the territory of "self" out of a one to ten?

Where are you in the territory of "health" out of one to ten?

Where are you in the territory of "wealth" out of one to ten?

Where are you in the territory of "relationships" out of one to ten?

Where are you in the territory of "business" out of one to ten?

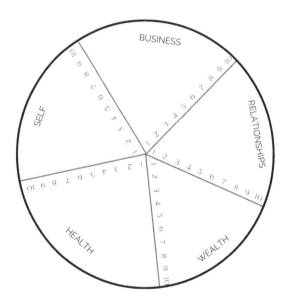

There's a chart here that looks like a pie graph. I want you to go ahead and make an arc on where you are and what numbers you've selected. So, for example, if you gave yourself a six on "self," you're going to go ahead and make a line at the number six and connect that piece of pie like you're slicing. Repeat this process for all of the 5

Territories. See the completed example for a reference. I'll add a few other examples at www.thepowerfulman.com/book

If you're like most men, then you have widely varying numbers for each territory. This is where you're at, in your five territories of your kingdom--this is a representation of your life.

Imagine, if you will, for a moment, that those five territories were really like a wagon wheel. Now attach that wheel to your wagon and set forth down the road of life. Is that going to be a bumpy ride or a smooth ride?

If you have all tens across all five territories (well, you wouldn't be reading this book, or you're lying to yourself about where you actually really are) then that road would be very smooth, and you would cruise along. However, if you have some threes in there and some eights and sixes mixed in, every time that wheel turns and hits a lower number, there will be a huge bump. In fact, that ride would be so bumpy for a lot of us that it would probably break the axles of that wagon.

Now I want you to imagine that the road that wagon is on is your life. Is that road going to be bumpy if things stay the same? Or is it going to be smooth?

I've been there, and when I first did this exercise, I thought to myself, "Man, this wagon isn't gonna go more than six inches before it breaks down."

But I did something that a lot of other people didn't do. I immediately went to work. I became determined that I was going to change things. I selected "relationships" as my number one priority in my five territories and I went after fixing that territory by giving myself the knowledge and skills necessary to save my marriage, so that part of my road could be as smooth as possible.

Lo and behold, as my marriage improved, all the other territories improved along with it. They say a rising tide lifts all boats. Well, I can tell you, in my experience working with thousands of men trying to save their marriage, when they focus on the relationships and get the coaching and skills they need to fix their marriages, that rising tide in relationships does lift all boats in all five territories. That doesn't mean you get to cruise. But it does mean you get to focus.

# The Live Like a King System

As stated before in this book, most of the men we work with have placed most of their focus, and thus their energy, towards the area of business. Business is only one of The 5 Territories, which we explained in a previous chapter.

When I was a child, I'd long to see my father when he was done with work. I didn't understand what he did, but I knew it was important, and thus work was important.

As men, society sells us the dream that if we put our heads down, work hard, and provide for our family, then in return, we will be loved and happy.

But that's not how it works out, is it?

As men, we focus on the territory of business because it gives us a sense of identity and significance. In fact, it's one of the first questions many people ask when they meet someone: - What do you do?

As times get tougher in our marriage and we feel that we're not being met with the love and respect we believe we deserve, we go to the place where we know we can be appreciated and made to feel important--our work.

By focusing on business, we often either cause or contribute to the issues we are having in our marriage. This is why we get to flip this focus around from business to self, so we can make continued and lasting progress.

The Live Like a King System organizes the 5 Territories in a sequential order, beginning with filling your cup (Self) so that you can overflow into others.

The territory of "business" goes from being the first territory focused on to the last. This doesn't mean you don't earn money. In fact, most men report to us that they end up making more while working less. A direct byproduct of their cups being filled.

Now, I know what you're saying because I've heard it a thousand times: "Doug, are you telling me I shouldn't work hard? Are you telling me to stop growing my business?"

No.

I love making money, and I love what I do for work. In fact, talking about business is one of my favorite things to do.

The problem arises when business is the only thing we focus on.

Instead of business being first, we're going to move "Self" to the front of the line, followed immediately by "Health."

These two areas are often the most neglected by men.

We're essentially taking the Five Territories and flipping them over.

CLEAN SLATE METHOD

This isn't a new concept.

Religious scholars tell me that this flipping of the 5 Territories is a fundamental piece of most all religious texts and has been taught since the beginning of recorded history.

So why isn't it talked about?

Why, instead, are we always sold this dream of "hustle and you'll be happy?"

Because it's much easier for me to sell you "things" that will make you happy, and in order for you to buy those things, you need to work hard to get the money to pay for them.

It's the same reason that public schools are designed the way they are today--to create good, loyal, and obedient factory workers.

If that model worked, you wouldn't be reading this book, and I wouldn't be sitting here trying to help you by writing it.

To be the King, you must build your castle, and a King must first take care of himself.

If you've been on a plane and actually listened to one of their safety talks, then you've heard them say something like this: "In the unlikely event of an emergency, oxygen masks may fall from the ceiling. Put your mask on first before assisting others."

Why do you think they say that?

It's because if you don't put your mask on first, you may pass out, and then you're no good to anyone.

However, if you put yours on first, then you can help countless others.

Think of the Live Like a King System as your oxygen mask. You must take care of yourself first before you can start to help others.

This was the most challenging part of the entire process for me, so I get it if this seems "selfish" or like something you're worried about taking on; however, I ask you to trust me. I've helped thousands of men like you get to the promised land, which is a crucial step in the process.

I also invite you to consider that the way you've been doing things hasn't worked or you wouldn't be reading this book right now, so let's try something new.

## One Destination - Two Paths

I was talking to one of our clients, a well-known public figure. He's someone you'd know if I told you his name, or at least it would sound familiar to you. I don't share that to impress you but to impress upon you what I'm about to share.

By all accounts, he was extremely successful.

Making money was easy for him--it always had been.

He was cover model fit, and looked ten years younger than his age.

He was funny, witty, and could talk about any subject.

But this man didn't have many friends.

Why?

Because men felt threatened by him.

You see, this man was on what we call the path of The Powerful Man.

My writing here won't do this explanation justice, so I'm going to shoot a video for you to explain what I'm about to explain here. If you, like me, are a visual person, go to www.thepowerfulman.com/onedestination, and you'll find a short video where I show you what I'm about to talk about.

You see, I believe we're all moving towards the same end goal. Some people call it success, others call it the dream, but we call it The Powerful Man. This is the ultimate version of you and what you desire.

Consider that destination to be at the top of a map for the purposes of this explanation.

At the bottom of the map is the starting point.

You'll notice that there are two paths at the starting point - the one on the left, which is the path most of us are on, and the one on the right, which is the path my client is on.

Both paths end up at the same destination--in theory.

Why do I say "in theory?"

Because most men never make it to the top. They know there is more inside for them, but they don't know how to access it. The most common description I hear is that it feels like no matter how hard they press on the gas, they feel as if their tires just keep spinning.

We start out on the path on the left, at the age of about 18 to 21, we start out with a bang. Many of us, myself included, start by trying to fill ourselves up by chasing women. Now, the order can be different for you, and I'll give you several examples here while using the most common for this illustration. Yours might have occurred in a different order or by another mechanism, but I'm sure you'll agree that the premise is the same.

When we start chasing women to fill us up, we give away our power to something external to ourselves. We get lost in the vortex that becomes this identity, which seems like a bottomless pit. Typically, something happens on that journey that spits us back down lower on the path.

What happens could be a breakup, getting a girl pregnant, getting caught cheating, or a whole slew of other issues.

The point is that we get stuck in what seems like a time warp, or eddy, constantly going in circles rather than on our way toward our goal.

Once we get out of this trap, we move on--until we get caught once again.

The next time it could be the trap of the hustle. We think that if we work longer and harder, then we'll make enough money to do XYZ, and then we'll be happy.

I did this, starting and running multiple companies, with the hope of retiring early to enjoy my life. I thought I could outwork those other guys, so I'll work seven days a week rather than doing the things I loved, only to find myself getting burnt out and losing my friends and relationships in the process.

Or perhaps for you, it was drugs, alcohol, gambling, prostitutes, or some other means of sedation.

They all have the same result. The same effect.

All these things tend to put us in a tailspin and shoot us back down toward the bottom of the path.

Sure, we inch our way up, and sometimes it feels like we're running, but ultimately, we burn it down or tell ourselves we got burned by someone or something outside of our control.

All the while, there on the other path, the "right path," is another man walking a windy but seemingly straight path compared to the one we're on.

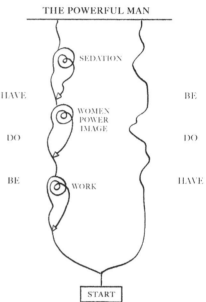

THE POWERFUL MAN

We look at that man, and we judge him.

"He probably inherited his business from his parents. He didn't have to work for it."

"Sure, he's in great shape, but I bet he's gay. It's easier for those guys."

"His marriage looks great, but I bet behind closed doors it's pitiful."

The list of excuses and blame I've heard could fill an entire book. I'm sure you've also heard your fair share of things like this from others as well. Perhaps, you've even caught yourself thinking them.

And I'm also sure that somewhere along your journey, a man on the other path, the right path, has walked across and offered you a helping hand or advice on how you could join him on the path he's on--the road less traveled.

He could have been a mentor, a church leader, a friend, or just a guy you met along your journey.

Chances are, you weren't ready to hear him, so you dismissed what he had to say, and he moved on.

And why wouldn't he move on, considering the things we men make up about guys who are doing the right things? Seeing someone else be successful where we aren't makes us feel bad about ourselves, so we put them down in a poor attempt to lift ourselves up.

This is why my client doesn't have many friends--he got on the right path early on in his life, and after reaching out to help others, he got tired of being burned, so he put his hand down and enjoyed his life by himself.

Well, I should say that he used to not have a lot of friends. He's now in The Brotherhood, a group of like-minded men who appreciate growth, adventure, and being around other amazing men. He knows he has brothers around him who are also working on bettering themselves, not by putting others down, but by lifting each other up.

The point is, ask yourself which path you've been on, and which path do you want to be on?

I was on the left-hand side most of my young life.

Despite doing better than most people around me, I got stuck in the eddies of women, work, and sedation more times than I care to admit.

It didn't mean I was weak or that there was anything wrong with me. I just didn't know better.

And yes, I can think of many times other men have reached across the other path to offer me a better way. I made up stories about how they must be wrong or that I could do it better because I was smarter, younger, or--insert any other story to make myself feel better about myself and my situation.

At The Powerful Man, we teach the path on the right without judging those on the left. And if you want to get your marriage to a place where your wife is constantly looking at you with love, respect, and admiration, then I suggest getting your behind over to the right-hand side--today.

Let's start by winning the day.

There have been many books and articles on "morning routines," and most of them will work in some capacity as long as they put you in the mindset of being proactive with your day instead of reactive. You get to dictate how the day goes, starting with what you do first thing in the morning.

At The Powerful Man, we call this process The Alpha Rise and Shine (ARS).

## The Alpha Rise and Shine (ARS)

How you start your day sets the scene for how your day goes, just like in business. I'm guessing you wouldn't show up to the office without a game plan for the day, week, month, or year?

If you did this, then chances are you wouldn't make much progress, and your business would end up running you instead of you running your business.

Instead of being a businessman, you'd become a firefighter, reacting to the flames as you saw them.

Well, the same is true of your day. If you start your day without taking control and setting the scene, then guess what?

Your day ends up running you.

Before you know it, you're coming home and walking through the door, already exhausted, with nothing left to give your loved ones, let alone yourself.

As the days, weeks, months, and even years pass, you continually deplete your cup. Eventually, you find yourself trying to pour from a nearly empty cup--it just doesn't work.

A common thing we hear from children and wives of men is that the man gives their work his best and then gives them the rest. That sucks!

Setting your day up strong is like baking a cake; a few key ingredients are required for it to have the maximum impact.

When you commit to doing this consistently, you shift from living outside-in to living inside-out.

You go from being a firefighter masquerading as an entrepreneur to being a full stack POWERFUL man, where your kingdom continues to rise as you do.

The "Alpha" in The Alpha Rise and Shine stands for Attune, Learn, Prioritize, Honor Your Body, and Accelerate. Let's break each of these down.

## Attune

Make no mistake about it, you are a finely-tuned machine. And just like a guitar, you must tune yourself daily to hit the right notes.

Start your day by drinking a large glass of room-temperature water upon waking. Bonus points if you add mineral salts.

Get outside and walk for 15 - 20 minutes, working up a light sweat.

Sunlight is vital to waking up your system and getting your body functioning. Even if it's dark outside, get out there and walk.

If you need to use a treadmill or walk around your house, that's fine, but make sure you've got the proper lighting to wake your body up.

The benefits of sunlight in the morning include increased energy, improved metabolism, improved nutrient utilization, and improved functioning of the organs and tissues of the body. It helps to regulate the autonomic nervous system, leading to increased alertness during the day and improved sleep at night.

After your walk, read your vision statement and imagine yourself living it--how does it feel?

Note: If you don't have a vision statement, or don't know how to write one, go to www.thepowerfulman.com/vision for free training from me on how to properly set up a vision statement that will guide you on your journey.

What can you see? How do you carry yourself?

An advanced way to connect with your vision is to combine it with movement. When you're ready, try incorporating this into your morning walk--talking to yourself about your vision, speaking it into existence as if you're living it NOW. Personally, I have recorded my vision statement so that I can listen to it when I run or even in the car. This allows me to stay focused on what matters to me in my life rather than allowing other people's priorities to take precedence.

Feel the feelings you'd feel, carry yourself in the way you do in your vision, and let the excitement, appreciation, and peacefulness flow.

Finally, go through your "Alpha Breath for Energy" breath practice--bonus points if you combine this with your morning walk.

NOTE - Avoid going on your mobile phone or laptop first thing in the morning.

## Learn

Learn for at least 15 minutes.

Learning is not consumption. Learning takes place when behavior changes.

Choose a relevant topic that's going to move you toward your vision. Bonus points if you learn content from this book, even if it means going over something you've already covered. Repetition is the driver of success.

As of the publishing of this book, we have over 700 audio and video trainings available absolutely free. If you're already enrolled in The Activation Method, then your coach will supply you with the best trainings to help you achieve your goals. Head over to www.thepowerfulman.com/book for more ideas and direction.

## Prioritize

Show me your calendar, and I'll show you your priorities.

Look at your day--does it match up to your vision? Is there time for you, your health, your relationships, and your business?

What are the top three things that you will get done today?

What can you do today to help bring you and your partner closer together? Perhaps it's simply taking care of YOU.

## Honor Your Body

Take the time to exercise.

You may classify your morning walk as your workout. However, if you're really ready to take your game to the next level, make a separate time to work out.

I highly recommend weight training.

Weight training is important for men because it can help maintain muscle mass and hormone levels, which can decline with age. Studies have shown that weight training with heavy loads, anywhere from one rep maximum to somewhere in the six to eight repetition range, can increase testosterone significantly. Additionally, weight training can help maintain muscular and bone health and can even be done with body weight if you don't have access to equipment.

Let's be real. A sexier you not only feels good when you look in the mirror, but it's also nice to get recognition from others. (hint: when you look good, you feel good, and when you feel good, you become more attractive to your partner--and other women).

## Accelerate

Have a cold shower. Start slow. At the end of your shower, turn the temperature down to cold for 30 seconds. At first, you might not be able to take it to the coldest. Build it up until you can be under the coldest temperature for two minutes.

Make sure you continue to breathe during this--the cold water might take your breath away, and that's normal. Continue to breathe in rhythmic cycles.

Put The Alpha Rise and Shine in the "brushing your teeth" category of life. This is something you do every day without question. Your self-care gets to be your priority.

OK, so we've nailed the morning and feel on top of the world. That's amazing, but what about at night?

Well, if you've heard me speak before, you'll know that I believe the morning starts at night. So, of course, we'll have to have an evening routine as well.

But first, we must ensure that we do not walk in the door carrying the stress of the day's work on our shoulders and then dump it on our loved ones.

We've all done it, and I'm as guilty as the next guy.

You come home after a long day, exhausted or stressed and anxious. The next thing you know, you find yourself snapping at your wife or dumping all the day's problems onto her lap as if you were vomiting your problems all over her. Now that's sexy, right?

Wrong.

We need to decompress after the work day--enter the Alpha Decompression.

## Alpha Decompression

Here's the reality: Different situations in your life require different versions of you. If you imagine a sports team, every player on the team plays a different position and has a different role. However, they all come together to achieve a common purpose.

It's the same thing for you and your life.

The vision you have for your life requires you to play different roles at different times, all of which come together and feed into you living your most powerful life.

Your wife wants you to be a lover and a leader, and your kids might want you to be the CFO (Chief Fun Officer), and your business may require you to be the visionary.

How do you shift between these different modes without compromising one for the others?

Well, The Alpha Rise & Shine Protocol will help get you ready for your role in business, whereas The Alpha Decompression Routine will get you ready to walk in through the door in the evening and connect with your wife and kids.

Are you familiar with martial arts?

Let's suppose you're a martial artist for a moment. At the end of your session, what happens?

You leave the floor, turn, bow to the dojo, turn around, and walk away.

This symbolizes that you've left your fighting energy on the floor and that you will not be taking it with you.

The Alpha Decompression Routine works in the same way. Use it at the end of your working day, as it is most effective when done before you walk through the door and see your family.

Experiment, enjoy, and commit!

Once again, we'll use the word "Alpha" as an acronym to help you remember. Alpha, in this case, stands for Attune, Lessons, Plan, Honor your wins, and Accept that the day is over.

Let's dive in.

The Alpha Decompression Process

## Attune

As we spoke about, you have different roles in your life requiring different things from you. Your wife wants the lover and leader, your kids want the CFO, and you might want to feel powerful, like a KING!

One of the fastest ways we've found to help men shift modes is by using the "Alpha Breath for Peace." Listen to the audio--that will attune you. You can find the audio at www.thepowerfulman.com/alphabreath.

NOTE - Avoid caffeine after two p.m.; otherwise, it will make it difficult for you to switch modes.

## Lessons

What have your lessons been today? Reflect, write them down, be with them, and appreciate your progress. Remember, things that don't go right aren't failures unless you don't learn from them.

Write down your lessons in your journal so you can continue to grow and lean on your own internal wisdom over time.

This will make you a stronger leader and a stronger person.

## Plan

Show me your calendar, and I'll show you your priorities. Plan your day tomorrow in alignment with Inside Out Living and plan the evening ahead--see it, feel it.

Do you have all your "rocks" on your calendar?

Did you schedule your Self-time?

Did you schedule your Relationship time?

If not, you better rethink your priorities.

If you don't own your calendar, you'll spend your life doing someone else's bidding. That's not what a Powerful Man does. Instead, he makes sure his calendar reflects those things most important to him.

If you need help determining what those things are, think of yourself as an old man sitting in a rocking chair reflecting on his life. What would that man be most proud of? Certainly not putting in more time in the office when he could have been living the life of his dreams, playing with his children, or making love to his wife.

## Honor Your Wins

You set the rules of this game, and you determine what it means to win. What if you set the rules of the game so that you could actually win it every day?

Write down at least five wins every single day.

Bonus points (I like bonus points) if you read over your wins each week.

Be with your wins, feel them, appreciate them, and appreciate yourself for the effort and risks you've taken and the challenges you've overcome.

## Accept That the Day Is Over

Today is done, and tomorrow is planned. There's nothing you can do now other than enjoy your evening, so go and do that. You've earned it.

All too often, as men, we sit and think about the problems of the day. We do this in an effort to solve them. This creates worry and anxiety.

Allowing the thoughts of the day to consume you also prevents you from being present with your family. And, you know what they say, the best present is your presence.

## The King isn't Needy

Want to know a surefire way to repel a woman? Be needy.

Yet almost all the men I encounter do just that--they become needy when their wife withdraws, further pushing them away.

What's worse is that most of these guys don't even recognize it when they're doing it.

Hey, I was in the same boat, so I get it.

As I've mentioned many times in this book, the first step is to understand what's happening so that you can make changes and course correct.

I teach this concept, about being needy, with an analogy.

My Dad has two cats. When I walk into his house, one of those cats is inevitably sitting on the couch.

I typically ignore the cat, sit down, and do my thing.

Guess what happens?

Within a few minutes, the cat gets up from its comfy perch, comes over, and rubs against me.

Again, I ignore it.

The cat then works harder to get my attention and affection and will paw at me to test the waters to see if it can sit on my lap.

Again, I ignore it.

The cat curls up in my lap, purring and allowing me to pet it with looks of affection.

Now, imagine what would happen if instead of coming, sitting down, and ignoring the cat when I entered the room, I instead got excited and walked quickly up to that cat, trying to pet it.

The cat would jump up and run away.

Let's say I decided to keep pursuing the cat, trying to get it to understand that I just wanted to pet it and make it feel good by scratching its ears.

The cat would run further away and probably hide somewhere, hoping I would go away and not come back.

Well, the cat in this example is your wife, and my guess, my friend, is that you are chasing her, trying to get her to see how amazing you are and get her acceptance.

Perhaps you are explaining to her how much you love her and why staying together is best for her.

Or, perhaps you're chasing her, trying to get her to have sex with you, only to find her uninterested.

You're being needy.

Shoot, we've all been there.

The sooner we recognize that we're being the guy chasing the cat, the sooner we realize that cats don't want to be chased. They want to be enticed and be around someone who doesn't require their presence.

It's a weird thing, but it's how attraction works.

You not only need polarity, but you also need to be so grounded within yourself as the king, or The Powerful Man, so that you don't need your partner, and thus you don't come across as needy.

The ironic thing about it is that in most cases, when we as men are doing our ARS, standing in our power, and are happy with who we are as men, our wives are more interested in being with us.

Why?

Because we're bettering ourselves. Our stock is rising. And we're not being like children trying to get mommy to fulfill our every need. That's gross. And as much as I hate to admit it, I did it when I was having problems in my marriage because being a "nice guy" is what we're taught.

It doesn't work. Instead of being a "nice guy," be a Powerful Man.

Dave's mornings went from sleeping in to getting up early with a pep in his step that everyone noticed. Dave began each day with his ARS (Alpha Rise and Shine).

He was now planning his day rather than reacting to it, which brought down his stress and anxiety. His productivity at work was more than doubled, and his wife was noticing a change in the way he was looking.

Sure, Dave was starting to lose some weight and show some muscles like he used to have, but that wasn't what his wife was noticing as much as the glow on Dave's face.

It certainly didn't hurt that Dave went from sitting on the couch with a dark cloud over his head to a man going after what he wanted in life—that is sexy!

Dave's stock was rising. Dave's wife, and her friends, were taking notice and Dave's wife was finding herself drawn to Dave once again.

# Taking Back Leadership

In every relationship, there needs to be a leader. This is evident in business, and often the founder or the CEO steps into this role, but it's also evident in sports when the team looks to the leader to take that final shot, demand the ball, or decide what the next play will be. This is also extremely relevant in your intimate relationships and in your family.

Often, when the relationship starts, most men take a leadership position. They initiate asking the woman out, usually initiate the first kiss, and often decide what will happen early on. But as the scales tip out of their favor, and bad feelings and discontent start to outweigh the good experiences they had previously, most men fall into more of a nice guy role.

They think that to make their wife happy, they have to do things around the house. They have to become subservient to her. Now, this is an unconscious decision. But when this happens, the woman feels unsafe. This is unsteady ground; she must move out of her femininity and into her masculinity, which for most women is not the natural or desired state to be in and as such, it becomes the cause of the wavering and instability in the marriage.

When this balance shifts, the woman must assume leadership. She starts to make decisions about the kids: where they go to school, what afterschool activities they have, what friends their kids have, which shows they watch on TV, and a myriad of other decisions.

The man stops making decisions altogether for fear of making the wrong decision or simply because he's given up so much of his autonomy in the relationship that he no longer cares.

A classic example is when a woman asks the man, "Where do you want to go for dinner?" And he replies, "I don't care, where do you want to go?" putting her back into her masculine and forcing her to make the decision for both of them.

Many women say that when they feel they have to take on this leadership role, they feel their husband is just another child they have to take care of, and they now feel unsafe around him. Seeing her husband as another child, or burden that drains her, is hardly the energy that is going to make your wife hot and bothered and want to get into the sack with you.

When most men hear that their wife doesn't feel safe, they are shocked because they think "well, I can protect her. She should feel safe with me. I would never hurt her or allow anyone else to hurt her."

The problem is that men are looking at this from a physical perspective rather than an emotional one. Yes, he will defend his wife against another man attacking them. However, this is not what his wife is talking about. She is saying that she doesn't feel emotionally safe because the man isn't in the dominant or Alpha leadership role. And thus, she has to do her job as well as his within the family.

What often happens for men is that they step into the role of leader of the family as this feels natural to them, but as soon as they're met with resistance from their partner, they step out of that role because they feel they may be in the wrong or they don't want to upset the applecart.

For example, you could find yourself in the leadership role, feeling strong, feeling great, but you and your wife get into an argument, or she cuts you down, and you then immediately retreat because you want to be the nice guy rather than erupting and causing a fight or an argument that might set your marriage back. So you go right into "nice guy syndrome," \or what we call "DEER mode," where you're defending, excusing, explaining, and reacting.

I want you to imagine there's a ship out at sea at night. Suddenly, a big storm rolls in and starts throwing the ship around like a ragdoll. The clouds cover any light that might have otherwise been available from the moon and the stars.

The captain of the ship sees a lighthouse in the distance, shining brightly. He knows that there are lots of rocks along this area of the coastline, so he quickly turns his ship towards the lighthouse so he can safely get out of the storm and navigate the rocks that if hit would certainly sink his ship.

The captain, still in peril, but somewhat hopeful with the lighthouse nearby, is dismayed when the lighthouse light goes out. "What do I do now?" the captain thinks to himself. Due to the impending rocks, he has no choice but to head back out to sea and face the storm.

The lighthouse comes back and once again relieved, the captain steers his ship towards the lighthouse to avoid the rocks. Once again, the light goes out.

This scenario repeats itself until the captain decides he can no longer trust that the lighthouse will remain on long enough for him to find safety, so he must head back out into the eye of the storm and find safe harbor elsewhere.

Now in this analogy, your wife is the captain of the ship at sea. When times get tough, as they often do, she is looking for somewhere she can go and feel safe. She is looking to get out of the storm--even if she herself helped create it.

She is looking for her lighthouse to guide her into safety.

As the captain of the ship, she will test the lighthouse's integrity. She will test to ensure that the lighthouse will always remain "on" no matter what happens.

These tests can be real or manufactured (remember the chapter on "shittests?"). When the tests come, if we go into DEER mode (defend, excuse, explain, react), then this is the same as the lighthouse that turns off its lights.

When you "turn off," she can no longer trust that you will be there for her, and thus she will not feel safe within the marriage. This causes many women to drift back out to sea, take control of their own fate and destiny as the captain of their boat, and search for another lighthouse they can trust. This other lighthouse can be a friend, a coworker, a family member, or, in many cases, another man.

The key here is to take back leadership and ensure that you are the lighthouse that shines brightly, always, never dimming or turning off your light.

With the tools we've already talked about, like the Triad of Connection, we want to set up many backup generators in your lighthouse so that you can shine brightly, and your wife can come in, even if a storm is crashing down on you or her and know that the leader of the home will always protect her.

Being the leader of the house doesn't mean being a jerk. It also doesn't mean your wife doesn't get a say or an opinion. That's not the way a true leader acts.

A leader leads by example, stands firm, sets boundaries, communicates them clearly, and also enforces them. A leader, like a lighthouse, is unmovable. They don't go into DEER mode.

They don't defend their actions because they're the leader. They don't react because they lead the family. They make decisions for their family and are in alignment with their family's values by reaching a consensus on what their family may need.

Ultimately, at the end of the day, somebody needs to be the leader of your family. Somebody needs to step up and take the shot. And this is what you get to do if you want to save your marriage. You get to once again step into that role and be the leader of your family. You get to once again find your groove and get your mojo back so that you can lead your family to prosperity, love, friendship, and better days. This will allow you to tip the scales back in your favor, and you'll have more control over what goes on in your daily life.

Just as in business, everybody needs to know who the leader is and who they should go to with questions. Often, men abdicate their power to their wives, especially over their children and the decisions to be made. This is your chance to jump back in. Find out what's going on with your children. Make your voice heard about what they're doing and what activities they're participating in. Decide what goes on in your house. Decide when dinner is served, when breakfast happens, and how rituals and community are formed around your home. It is extremely important for you to set the tone and be involved in these decisions and not just saying "oh, my wife takes care of that." That is no longer acceptable. For most guys, this attitude is what got them here in the first place, and with that said, what got you here won't get you "there."

Your wife isn't looking for you to make every decision or be authoritative. She's simply looking for a partner who can step in and help out and help run the family and the marriage as a union. Being more involved in day-to-day decisions, running your household, and running your marriage will relieve your wife's burden and stress by reassuring her that she has a true partner to whom she can turn and someone she can trust again to help her make decisions and ensure that what she's doing is best for the family.

In every set of two people, there will always be an alpha and a beta. You get to decide which role you're going to play. But I can tell you with certainty that if you want your marriage to work, let alone thrive, you need to take the Alpha role.

At The Powerful Man, we teach our men to have this assured confidence that they can bring into any situation, especially their marriage. This is not cockiness. This is strictly confidence in knowing who you are as a man and the value you bring to the table. This confidence allows you to shift the dynamic in your family and shift energy that will help you tip those scales and keep them tipped in your favor, where good experiences and good memories far outweigh the bad ones.

When your wife trusts you once again and feels safe around you. She'll start to lean into you a lot more. Again, think of the lighthouse analogy. A lighthouse that turns itself on and off without notice cannot be trusted. In fact, it's a useless lighthouse when you think about it. So often, men will show up strong and confident one moment, and then, when our wives trigger us or give us a "shittest," we crumble. Thus, like the lighthouse turning our light off. This is the last thing your wife wants, desires, or needs. She needs a lighthouse that shines brightly regardless of the storm coming at it, regardless of the time of day, and regardless of the situation.

This is often why successful men complain that they find out that their wife is having an affair emotionally or physically with a lesser man. Often it's because this "lesser man" is showing up as the Alpha and is showing up consistently. It's time for you to take your leadership back.

# Being Decisive

Being decisive is easy, right?

Well, all too often, when men enter "nice guy" mode, they stop being decisive and making decisions because they feel like they are on unstable ground. As mentioned in the last chapter, the classic scene is deciding what to eat for dinner. It goes something like this: Your wife asks, "What do you want to eat tonight?" You answer, "I don't know, what do you want to eat?" She answers. "I don't care." You answer, "I don't care either." And then you spend the time mulling around, trying to figure out where to go.

Now let's see how an Alpha would answer the situation. Your wife turns to you and says, "Where do you want to eat tonight?" The Alpha says, "I've already got reservations at the Mexican restaurant on Fifth Street. Be ready at six p.m., and I'd love it if you wore that blue dress you look so good in." Period.

The difference here is that the man in the second example, the Alpha, is taking the leadership role, and part of being a leader is being decisive. He doesn't have to always have the reservations booked, but he should make a decisive decision on where to go or at least provide two options for his wife.

One of women's top complaints about their marriage is the feeling that they have to make all the decisions. This takes them out of their femininity and puts them in a state of masculinity. When they're in a state of masculinity, they feel out of control. And it's a state that simply doesn't feel good for them. It's not sexy. They want a man who will be decisive, who will take charge, and allow them to slip into their femininity and enjoy the ride.

Where have you not taken control of the decision-making process in your life and in your relationships?

Have you hemmed and hawed about the rules around your family? Perhaps not being decisive about whether your marriage is worth working on or not. For many men reading this book, you're still trying to decide if you want a divorce or if you want to save your marriage.

For others, you're deciding if coaching or a program is a good fit for you, but you haven't decided yet. And being on the fence is the worst place to be. It's like having one foot on the dock, and one foot on the boat as the boat starts to set off. You can stand on the dock and play it safe, or you can jump on the boat and enjoy the ride wherever it goes, or you can do what most men do and keep one foot on the dock and one foot on the boat until they look like some yogi doing the splits until they often fall in the water and end up nowhere.

Start being decisive today. If you haven't exercised your decisive muscles, start small. Make a commitment right now to read a specific number of chapters of this book each week; just like building any muscle in the gym, the decision-making process can take time to build if you haven't used the decision muscle in a long time.

Start with micro-decisions and slowly work your way up to bigger ones. But hey, you can also just decide to jump in with both feet on that boat today and sail off into the sunset while watching the old DEER version of yourself fade away. The choice is yours.

Let's take your marriage, for example: Do you want to be married to your wife? Yes or no? I don't want to hear the story or anything else. If the answer is no, then it's time for you to get out. If the answer's yes, it's time for you to go all in. Either way, it's time to get off the fence or as some say, it's time to shit or get off the pot.

What else are you on the fence about? Is it about working out? Is it about having a conversation with your wife about something you want to do? Perhaps you're on the fence as to whether or not to commit to your Alpha Rise and Shine or your Alpha Decompression? Perhaps it's about joining The Activation Method. Whatever it is for you, make a decision—a yes or no decision, and then move on.

Don't worry so much about the consequences of your decision but rather that you're being decisive. When you're decisive, you can move forward, even if you're moving forward in the wrong direction. It's better than being stagnant, spinning your wheels, and wasting your energy. Moving forward allows you to be more in the WOLF zone. Remember that WOLF is an acronym for Wise, Open, Loving, and Fierce. There's wisdom in being decisive. But it also brings out the fierceness of the wolf. The fierceness allows the wolf to be the leader, to rise above the chaos, and to move forward when times are hard. It's this decisiveness that people look to in the leader, even when they're wrong. In the military, when they're looking for somebody to take on a leadership role, decisiveness is one of the top indicators of leadership because men will follow a decisive leader even if they think he is wrong. This is because he's so confident and he's able to make decisions quickly.

Make a list of items you have not made a decisive decision on yet. Once you have your list, go through that list and make a decision one way or another. This process will not only help you to become more decisive, but it will also clear up the clutter in your brain and allow you to be more effective in all areas of your life.

As Dave's confidence grew, he started being more decisive at home. At first, his wife looked at him strangely and gave him a fair share of shittest, but Dave was now able to recognize those for what they were and handled them like a Powerful Man, turning them from arguments to foreplay.

Dave brought the same level of decisiveness he had at work into the home but added an element of light-hearted fun to ease any tension. Of course, he considered everyone in his decision and was willing to change his mind.

Dave noticed his wife would be more relaxed in the evenings and started to defer to Dave when it came to decisions around family events and the kids. Sure, she still had strong opinions, but Dave married her because she was so smart, so why would he ignore her ideas?

Instead, Dave led from the front and guided his wife along the journey of their marriage.

# Date Night

When was the last time you took your wife on a date? Really, when was the last time you took her out on a proper date? For most married people, these times are fewer and farther between. When kids get added to the mix, especially young ones, date nights, let alone sleep, seem to be far-reaching.

When you first started your relationship, dating was the most important part. Because this allowed you time to connect with each other. This allows you time to get to know each other and feel that intimate bond. And over time, you became more like roommates. It became like a business decision to be together. The logistics of running the family and running daily life were the only conversations you ended up having besides the fights.

And over time, the time between intimacy grew further and further apart. Date Night brings back that excitement, brings back those conversations, and allows you to get intimate, possibly physically, but certainly allows you to get intimate emotionally.

You are not the same man that married your wife. You've changed over time; your experiences have hardened or softened you, you've learned new things, and you feel differently. Your wife is much the same. But have you taken time to get to know the new her? I mean,

A Man's Guide on How to Save Your Marriage

gosh, could you imagine allowing the 21-year-old version of yourself to run your life today? Absolutely not. So you've got to expect that you've changed a lot, and so has your wife. If you're not doing regular date nights, there's no way for you to know what's going on in her world.

You probably haven't sprinkled enough mystery and fun to allow intimacy in your marriage. And this is an indicator of a failing or successful marriage. Remember what I said earlier? The only difference between you, her husband, and her brother or father is that you are intimate with your wife, and they are not. Your wife probably loves her brother or a father or another male companion that she's not having sex with. But the difference between you, her husband, is in theory, you guys are having sex together. Other than that, you're just good friends. And unfortunately for most of us, if you're reading this book, the friendship has also been diminished. And now you just have a roommate, possibly kids, and a commitment and a promise you made.

Date Night allows you to bring this back to full fruition. And if you've been following the steps in this book or our program, The Activation Method, you'll find that date night also allows you to showcase the new you. The Alpha, the leader, the man, and the lighthouse your wife has always wanted.

Here are some reasons why date nights are important for maintaining a healthy and strong relationship:

1. They help to keep the romance alive. Date nights give you the chance to dress up, go out, and enjoy each other's company without the distractions of everyday life. It's a chance to focus on each other and show your partner how much they mean to you.

2. They allow for deeper conversations and connection. Date nights provide a chance for you and your partner to have more in-depth conversations and really listen to each other. It's an opportunity to share your thoughts and feelings and to get to know each other on a deeper level.

3. They can help to reduce stress and improve overall well-being. Taking a break from the daily grind can help to reduce stress and improve overall well-being. When you're with your partner, you're able to relax and enjoy each other's company, which can have a positive impact on your mental and emotional health.

4. They can strengthen your bond. Date nights give you the chance to strengthen your bond with your partner and reaffirm your commitment to each other. They help to remind you of why you fell in love in the first place and can help to reignite the spark in your relationship.

5. They can help to prevent boredom and monotony. It's easy to fall into a routine and do the same things over and over again in a relationship. Date nights give you the opportunity to try something new and shake things up. This can help to prevent boredom and monotony in your relationship and keep things exciting.

6. They can improve communication. Date nights provide a dedicated time for you and your partner to talk and really listen to each other. By taking the time to have in-depth conversations, you can improve your communication and understand each other better. This can be especially important if you've been experiencing any communication breakdowns in your relationship.

7. They can foster appreciation and gratitude. When you take the time to plan and enjoy a date night with your partner, it shows that you value them and your relationship. It's an opportunity to express your appreciation and gratitude for each other and to let your partner know how much they mean to you.

8. They can help to resolve conflicts. Date nights can provide a more relaxed and neutral environment for discussing any conflicts or issues that may have arisen in your relationship. By taking the time to talk things through and listen to each other's perspectives, you can work towards resolving any conflicts and strengthening your bond.

So let's get into the logistics of what makes a good date night. The first is frequency. I recommend having at least one date night per week. For some people, especially those with young kids who don't have family around, this can be really tough. I get it. I was there too. I recommend you go out of your way to find babysitters, nannies, or anybody else who can help you watch the kids while you and your wife go out--even if it's only for a few hours. The time spent together is worth the investment.

I've heard guys tell me that a nanny is too expensive. Yet they were on the verge of divorce. When I asked them to sit down and calculate what their divorce would cost them just financially, the numbers were astronomically out of proportion to what the expense would be to have a nanny or a babysitter come in, help out around the house, and give them time to spend with their wives. It was a no-brainer, let alone the emotional costs of a divorce and separation and the toll it takes when you have children and your own identity.

Make date night a priority.

As we talked about in the chapter on leadership, this is where you get to take control of when date night happens, and what date night looks like.

Some couples prefer to switch back and forth on who decides what happens on date night, so the burden isn't always on the husband. However, I'm going to recommend that you decide where you're going to have date night each time, and that you add mystery and spice to it. On your date night, you want to find something fun. Look at your local paper, look online, find one of the Facebook groups (or other social media networks) that exist for every community, and see what's happening in your town. Find something fun and engaging that you enjoy. Ideally, it's something your wife also enjoys. It's essential that this is not something only she would want to do and that you are not just going along for the ride. That's what a nice guy does. That's a beta move. We want to find something that you love to do and that she will also enjoy.

So, for example, I love stand-up comedy. My wife likes it, but it wouldn't be her first choice. However, if I'm arranging date night, and we are going through a hard time, I would arrange for us to see a stand-up comedy show. Why, you ask? Well, if I'm not having a great time, then no one else will have a good time either.

It reminds me of hosting a party. You can go to a house party where the food is expertly catered, the house is immaculately clean, yet if the host is running around stressed, no one is having a good time. However, if you went to a house party where there was pizza sitting on the table from the local pizza shop and the house was clean, but messy, you wouldn't care as long as the host was having a good time. It's their energy that dictates the fun.

I've had just as much fun, if not more fun, at people's homes sitting on the floor laughing as I have had at some of the best restaurants in the world with a host that is stressed and not enjoying themselves.

Be the CFO on your date - the Chief Fun Officer. (For more on becoming the CFO, head to www.thepowerfulman.com/book)

Next, we want to pick a place. Typically, date night revolves around dinner, drinks, etc. Find out what restaurants or venues are open in your area for the date and time you've selected for your date night. Make reservations. Tell them that something special is occurring—an anniversary, or that you're taking your wife out on the first date in a long time.

Ask the restaurant to make something special; make the night special. It could be as simple as having a candle on the table or a little note. This will show her that you've assumed leadership and are planning ahead of time rather than reacting. You have stepped into the lighthouse, and you're taking an active role in dictating the path that your marriage is on.

Once you know what you're going to do, where you're going to go, as well as the day and the time, then it's time to invite your wife out for the date. It may go something like this. "Hey, baby, I want to take you out this Thursday. I got a babysitter to come to watch the kids. I need you to be ready at five p.m. We're going to be doing something somewhat active, so wear a pair of jeans, tennis shoes, and a shirt, and I'll come pick you up at the house."

You'll notice that I didn't ask if she wanted to go on a date with me. I didn't ask her where she wanted to go. I also assured her that I had taken care of her roles and responsibilities and the safety of the family. So all her stresses and worries are over.

I also did not tell her what we would do or where we would go. Now she may ask, and you may want to tell her some things, but I recommend you keep some mystery depending on where you are in your marriage. This may not be an option; she may not trust you enough to give you that authority yet. You may have to divulge a little bit more than you want to, but try to keep a bit of mystery, so she has some anticipation leading up to the date night.

This is where you're going to get some polarity. Stay in your masculine, open doors for her, act like the king and treat her like the queen and watch her melt into her feminine energy. Congratulations, you've achieved polarity!

I put together an eBook on how to set up the perfect date night which you can grab over at www.thepowerfulman.com/book

Our man Dave sent his wife a text to start off their first date night: Tuesday. I've got a babysitter, and I'm taking you out. Be ready to go at six p.m. Wear the black dress with the black heels. I'll be home to pick you up just before.

Dave showed up to the house at 5:55 p.m. to find a gorgeous woman, his wife, waiting in anticipation for what was to come.

Dave's wife asked "What are we doing? Where are we going?" To which Dave smoothly replied, "Don't worry about it, babe, I've got you covered."

The smile on Dave's wife could be seen for miles. What was about to happen? She thought.

Dave had made reservations at a hip little restaurant not too far from their house. He told them it was a special occasion and had asked for a window seat and a bottle of sparkling wine to be waiting at the table when they arrived.

As they sat down, his wife looked in shock, as it seemed that everything had been set up ahead of time. This was a new experience for Dave and his wife. "Who is this man?" Dave's wife thought to herself. "I love it!"

Dave took the initiative of ordering dinner for both of them and when dinner was over, Dave escorted his date back to the car and told her the night was just beginning.

Dave took her to a nightclub where a local band was playing and after being seated, Dave boldly stood up, took her hand, and brought her to the dance floor. Although Dave wasn't a particularly good dancer, he didn't care. Dave was focused on the woman he loved--she got all his attention… and she ate it up.

I won't go into details about what happened after the concert out of respect for Dave's wife, but let's just say they had a lot of fun that night!

# Riding Off into the Sunset

Saving your marriage starts with saving yourself. What I mean by that is that you need to get yourself back into your most powerful state as a man. This doesn't mean you beat your chest and walk around like some arrogant asshole.

No, being a Powerful Man means you embrace the WOLF by being Wise, Open, Loving, and Fierce.

I've had the privilege of witnessing thousands of men follow The Powerful Man's path, save their marriages, and turn them into more than they ever imagined possible.

At the same time, these men also connected on a deeper level with their children, friends, and community.

These men were born to be leaders--just like you.

You will be tested.

I did an entire Masterclass on how to handle these tests for the men in our Brotherhood program, and each of these men commented that they often got the most testing from their wives when they started to show up in their powerful selves once again.

So why would your wife test you when you start to show up in a way that she's been longing for you to show up all these years?

She needs to know it's real. She needs to know that this isn't some fly-by-night change and that the real powerful man she married is back, and he will stay. She's probably afraid that if she opens her heart completely to you, she'll be disappointed and hurt.

So, she needs to test you. Test your resolve. Are you going back into DEER mode, or will you continually be the lighthouse to guide her to safe shores no matter how severe the storm?

This is a process. You've taken the first step, and I commend you for that.

Most men won't read a book on how to better themselves, let alone take action. You are my kind of guy--someone who wants to better themselves not only for themselves but also for others.

There's a lot to what we teach at The Powerful Man that goes into becoming what we call "Activated." I'm not telling you that because I want you to sign up for the program. I hate when I buy a book that's clearly just designed to sell me the next thing. This is not that kind of book. But I'm also not going to BS you either, because I'm not that kind of coach or mentor.

There's only so much I can put down on paper. That's why, as of this writing, we have over 700 free podcasts talking about subjects like this. Nothing is hidden or withheld; it's just easier for me to talk about them than it is to sit at a keyboard and type it out.

I share that with you because I want you to go in with your eyes wide open and understand that although there's a lot here, this is just the beginning, my friend. I hope you choose to take that as an opportunity for growth and maintain a positive outlook on what's to come.

Your stock is rising, and regardless of whether you and your wife stay together, and I do hope you are able to make it, please remember that you are worthy.

My wife coaches women, and 100% of the women she works with talk about wanting to be with a man who is bettering himself. You are that man.

Should you choose to continue your journey with The Powerful Man movement, I hope to see you at an event so I can look you in the eyes and shake your hand.

The world needs more powerful men like you.

Thank you for being you.

If you're interested in finding more about The Powerful Man movement and the programs we offer, head over to www. thepowerfulman.com I'd love to see you at one of our events and have the opportunity to hear your story.

In your corner,

Doug

# Glossary of Terms

## (Please feel free to add!)

**Alpha:** "Alpha" typically refers to a mindset or approach that emphasizes confidence, assertiveness, and leadership qualities. It is not meant to suggest domination or control over one's partner, but rather a healthy level of self-assuredness and self-respect that can help build attraction and trust in a relationship.

For married businessmen looking to improve their relationships, embracing an "alpha" mindset might involve taking initiative in planning romantic dates or activities, communicating clearly and directly with their partner about their needs and desires, and showing appreciation and affection in ways that feel authentic and meaningful. It may also involve addressing any underlying issues or conflicts in the relationship, such as trust or communication problems, and working together with their partner to find solutions and build a stronger, more fulfilling partnership. Ultimately, the goal of adopting an "alpha" mindset is to cultivate a positive, confident, and loving energy that can help reignite the spark and deepen the connection between partners.

**Beta:** The term "beta" is often used to describe a more passive, accommodating, or submissive approach to interacting with one's partner.

While being "beta" is not inherently bad or negative, it may be problematic if it involves constantly deferring to one's partner, avoiding conflict or confrontation, or failing to take initiative in the relationship. In some cases, a "beta" approach can lead to feelings of resentment, frustration, or disconnection in the relationship.

**Lighthouse:** The concept of a lighthouse is often used as an analogy at The Powerful Man to describe the importance of being grounded and consistent in one's life and relationships. A lighthouse is a strong and steady presence that serves as a guide for ships at sea, helping them navigate safely to their destination.

Similarly, a man who embodies the qualities of a lighthouse is someone who is grounded and consistent in his thoughts, words, and actions. He is reliable and trustworthy, and he consistently provides guidance and support to those around him, particularly his partner in a marriage.

One of the key qualities of a lighthouse is that it does not try to save the boats at sea, but rather it guides them to safety. In the same way, a man who embodies the qualities of a lighthouse does not try to fix or solve every problem that comes his way, but rather he provides guidance and support to his partner, helping her navigate the challenges and difficulties of life.

Another key quality of a lighthouse is that its light shines brightly and never turns off, regardless of the circumstances. Similarly, a man who embodies the qualities of a lighthouse is someone who remains steadfast and consistent in his values and beliefs, even in the face of adversity or difficult situations. He is a beacon of light for those around him, providing a sense of direction and stability even in turbulent times.

Overall, the concept of a lighthouse is a powerful reminder of the importance of being grounded, consistent, and reliable in one's life and relationships. By embodying these qualities, a man can become a true leader and guide for those around him and create a strong and fulfilling relationship with his partner.

**DEER:** The way in which most married men show up in relationships and thus become the Beta. DEER stands for Defend, Excuse, Explain, and React, and it is often used to describe behaviors that are associated with a defensive or reactive posture in relationships. When individuals engage in DEER behaviors, they may feel the need to defend themselves, make excuses for their actions, explain their behavior, or react emotionally to criticism or feedback.

For example, a married man who engages in DEER behaviors may feel defensive when his partner expresses dissatisfaction with their relationship, and may respond by making excuses for his behavior, explaining why he acted a certain way, or becoming reactive and emotional in response to criticism. These behaviors can create a negative cycle in the relationship, as they can make it difficult for both partners to communicate effectively and work together to address issues and concerns.

**WOLF:** The concept of WOLF refers to the way in which a powerful man shows up in his life and relationships. The term WOLF is actually an acronym for four key qualities that are associated with a powerful and fulfilling life: Wise, Open, Loving, and Fierce.

Here's a breakdown of each of these qualities:

Wise: A powerful man who embodies wisdom is someone who is able to make sound decisions, learn from past experiences, and think critically about his life and his relationships. A wise man is someone who seeks knowledge and understanding and is willing to grow and evolve over time.

Open: Being open means being willing to explore new ideas, experiences, and perspectives. A powerful man who is open is someone who is receptive to feedback, willing to listen to others, and able to adapt to changing circumstances.

Loving: A powerful man who embodies love is someone who is compassionate, caring, and empathetic. He is able to connect with others on a deep emotional level and is willing to show vulnerability and share his feelings with those around him.

Fierce: Finally, a powerful man who is fierce is someone who is willing to stand up for what he believes in, take risks, and pursue his goals with passion and determination. He is someone who is confident and assertive and is not afraid to take bold action when necessary.

By embodying these qualities, a powerful man can show up in his life and relationships with strength, clarity, and purpose. He can build deep connections with those around him, pursue his goals with passion and determination, and live a life that is both fulfilling and meaningful.

**TAR:** TAR, which stands for The Alpha Reset, is a transformational in-person event offered by The Powerful Man company. The event takes place over three full days and is designed to help men break through their self-limiting beliefs, overcome their fears, and unlock their full potential.

At TAR, men have the opportunity to work with experienced coaches and mentors who provide guidance and support as they navigate the challenges and obstacles that have been holding them back. The event includes a variety of activities, including workshops, group discussions, and physical challenges, all designed to help men step outside their comfort zones and push themselves to new levels of growth and transformation.

Although many men who attend TAR describe it as the most important event of their lives, the specifics of the event are generally not discussed in detail. This is because TAR is treated much like Fight Club - the first rule of TAR is that you do not talk about TAR. This is partly because the experience of TAR is unique to each individual, and it is difficult to fully describe the transformational journey that each man goes through.

However, what can be said is that TAR is a powerful and transformative experience that has helped countless men break free from their limitations and become the best version of themselves. Through the intensive coaching and support provided at TAR, men are able to discover their true purpose and potential and develop the tools and strategies they need to achieve their goals and create the life they truly desire.

**Engaged Indifference:** Engaged indifference refers to the ability to actively participate and engage in conversations, negotiations, and conflicts while maintaining emotional balance and detachment from personal emotions. It involves recognizing and acknowledging one's own feelings and those of others involved, but not allowing these emotions to define or control one's actions. Instead, individuals practicing engaged indifference remain focused on the bigger picture, long-term goals, and objective decision-making, without becoming overly attached to specific outcomes or taking things personally. By adopting engaged indifference, professionals can navigate challenging situations, manage conflicts, negotiate effectively, foster collaboration, and cultivate trusting relationships based on respect and integrity.

**TAM:** The Activation Method is a proven methodology facilitated by a training coach, that guides a married man step-by-step through the process of saving their marriage and bringing the love and respect back into their wife's eyes.

**Triggered:** The term "triggered" is often used to describe a strong emotional reaction to a particular event, situation, or statement that may be rooted in past experiences, insecurities, or unresolved conflicts. This reaction can be intense and overwhelming and may lead to a breakdown in communication or a disconnection between partners.

**Shittest:** A "shit test" is a term used to describe a test performed by one partner in a relationship to assess the other's response or reaction. This is often done to gauge their partner's competence, confidence, or character. While commonly used in pickup artistry and seduction communities, shit tests can occur in any relationship.

**Triad of Connection:** The Triad of Connection is a set of three tools developed by The Powerful Man for their flagship program, The Activation Method. It includes the Clean Slate Method, the Hidden Motives Technique, and the Live Like a King System. These tools work together to shift a sexless marriage to one where the wife looks at her husband with love, respect, and admiration. The Clean Slate Method allows couples to start from scratch in their relationship, wiping away negative experiences and feelings. The Hidden Motives Technique allows a wife to be seen and heard, drawing her towards her husband effortlessly. The Live Like a King System reinforces behavior patterns and prevents slipping back into negative modes, ensuring the scales in the relationship stay in the husband's favor indefinitely.

**Powerful Man:** Being a Powerful Man refers to a mindset and way of being that prioritizes personal growth, taking action, and being a positive influence in the world. It means taking ownership of one's life and choices and striving to constantly improve oneself in all areas of life, including health, relationships, career, and personal development.

A Powerful Man is not defined by external factors like wealth or status, but rather by his inner strength, resilience, and ability to lead with purpose and integrity. He takes responsibility for his actions and decisions and is committed to being a positive force in the lives of those around him. A Powerful Man is not afraid to be vulnerable and is willing to confront his fears and limitations in order to grow and become a better version of himself.

**Clean Slate Letter:** A Clean Slate Letter is a letter written by a person to their partner or spouse, expressing their remorse for past mistakes or hurtful actions, and asking for forgiveness in an effort to start fresh and move forward in the relationship. The letter is meant to be a sincere and honest expression of regret, without making excuses or shifting blame, and it is often used as part of a healing process in couples therapy or marriage counseling. The Clean Slate Letter can serve as a powerful tool to help repair and rebuild trust in a relationship and can help both partners let go of past grievances and begin anew with a clean slate.

**Alpha Rise and Shine (ARS):** The Alpha Rise and Shine (ARS) is a morning routine that helps individuals take control of their day and set the scene for success. The name "Alpha" stands for Attune, Learn, Prioritize, Honor Your Body, and Accelerate. The routine involves drinking a large glass of water, walking outside, reading a vision statement, practicing an Alpha

Breath for Energy, learning something relevant for at least 15 minutes, prioritizing tasks for the day, and taking time to exercise, preferably weight training. By committing to the ARS consistently, individuals shift from living outside-in to living inside-out, leading to a more powerful and fulfilling life.

**Alpha Decompression:** Alpha Decompression is a term used by The Powerful Man to describe a process that helps high-performing men unwind, relax and recharge after intense periods of work or stress. The goal of Alpha Decompression is to help men disconnect from work and other responsibilities, allowing them to fully relax and recharge their batteries. This process is especially important for Alpha men, who are typically high achievers and have a tendency to be constantly working or thinking about work. Alpha Decompression may involve activities such as meditation, mindfulness, exercise, nature walks, reading, or any other activity that helps men relax and recharge. The idea is that by taking the time to decompress, men can come back to their work and personal lives with renewed energy, focus, and creativity.

**Polarity:** Refers to the dynamic between partners in terms of their masculine and feminine energies. This does not necessarily mean that one partner must be entirely masculine and the other entirely feminine, but rather that the balance of energies between partners creates a dynamic tension and attraction that can help to reignite the spark and deepen the connection in the relationship.

For example, a married man who feels stuck in a rut in his relationship may benefit from exploring his own masculine energy and finding ways to express this in the relationship. This might involve taking initiative in planning date nights or romantic getaways, communicating confidently and directly with his partner, and showing strength and stability in the face of challenges.

At the same time, the man's partner may benefit from exploring and embracing her own feminine energy, which might involve being more receptive and open to her partner's advances, expressing her feelings and emotions more freely, and nurturing the relationship through acts of love and kindness.

Ultimately, the goal of cultivating polarity in a relationship is to create a healthy balance of energies that feels authentic and fulfilling for both partners. By embracing and expressing their unique energies in a way that supports and complements one another, married men can build a deeper and more fulfilling connection with their partner.

**The Brotherhood (TBH):** The Brotherhood (TBH) is a year-long high-level mastermind group designed for businessmen who have completed The Activation Method program. The program is focused on epic growth, epic adventure, and working with epic men to help members achieve their full potential.

The Brotherhood is led by a coach who works with a small group of men to raise the bar in all five territories: self, health, wealth, relationships, and business. Through weekly education and growth courses, members are provided with the tools and strategies they need to achieve success in each of these areas.

In addition to the weekly courses, The Brotherhood also provides accountability and office hours where members can meet other like-minded men and continue to grow. This community aspect is a critical component of the program, as it allows members to connect with others who share similar goals and values, and to support each other on their journey to success.

One of the unique features of The Brotherhood is the two life-changing trips that members embark on each year. These trips are designed to be epic adventures that push members outside their comfort zones and provide opportunities for growth and transformation. They may include activities such as hiking, camping, rafting, or other outdoor adventures, as well as workshops and training sessions focused on personal and professional development.

Overall, The Brotherhood is a powerful and transformative program that provides businessmen with the tools, resources, and support they need to achieve their full potential and create a life of epic growth and adventure. By working together in a small group setting and committing to ongoing growth and development, members of The Brotherhood are able to achieve remarkable results and build lifelong relationships with other like-minded men.

**Hidden Motives Technique:** The Hidden Motives Technique is a communication technique that helps men better communicate to their wives their underlying emotional needs and desires. It is designed to help men validate their wives in a way that allows them to feel seen, heard, and desired, which can improve the quality of their relationship.

The technique involves asking open-ended questions that allow the wife to express her feelings and needs, without being defensive or judgmental. By using this technique, the husband can gain a deeper understanding of his wife's perspective, which can help him to respond in a more compassionate and supportive way.

The Hidden Motives Technique is especially useful in situations where there is conflict or tension in the relationship. By focusing on the wife's underlying emotional needs, rather than the surface-level issues, the husband can often resolve conflicts more quickly and effectively. This technique can also strengthen the emotional bond between the husband and wife, as it promotes open and honest communication.

Overall, the Hidden Motives Technique is a powerful tool for improving communication and intimacy in a marriage, and it can be a valuable addition to any couple's toolkit.

**Collecting Berries:** Collecting berries is a metaphor used in relationship counseling to describe the process of actively listening to a woman's daily experiences and emotions, without interruption or judgment. The metaphor comes from the idea that women, in their natural feminine state, are like gatherers who collect berries and bring them back to the tribe. In the context of a relationship, "collecting berries" means allowing the woman to express herself fully and release any emotional baggage she may be carrying, so that she can feel more present and connected with her partner. It's an essential part of building intimacy and trust in a relationship, as it shows that the partner values and respects the woman's experiences and emotions.

**Two Wolves:** The story of the two wolves is a Native American legend that symbolizes the battle between good and evil within each individual. It tells of a grandfather who explains to his grandson that there are two wolves fighting inside him: one represents anger, envy, sorrow, regret, greed, arrogance, self-pity, guilt, resentment, inferiority, lies, false pride, superiority, and ego; while the other represents joy, peace, love, hope, serenity, humility, kindness, benevolence, empathy, generosity, truth, compassion, and faith. The story emphasizes the importance of feeding the positive wolf while starving the negative one to live a fulfilling and harmonious life.

**Shadow Stickman:** The shadow stickman is an unconscious aspect of a person's personality that includes both positive and negative qualities. It can manifest as defensive or negative behaviors in relationships and can be a barrier to achieving true intimacy. Understanding and identifying the shadow stickman can lead to greater self-awareness and improved relationships.

**Keystone Habit:** A keystone habit is a habit that has a positive and cascading effect on other areas of one's life. It is a habit that, once established, can lead to the development of other good habits, which in turn can lead to the improvement of one's overall life. Keystone habits have a significant impact on a person's behavior and mindset, and they can create a domino effect that leads to positive change in various aspects of life, such as health, relationships, career, and personal growth. Examples of keystone habits include regular exercise, meditation, reading, and planning.

**Be-Do-Have:** "Be Do Have" is a philosophy that emphasizes the importance of first developing a certain mindset or way of being, then taking appropriate actions, and finally achieving desired results or possessions. The idea is that by focusing on who you are being, you can more effectively take action and achieve your goals. This approach suggests that success comes from within and is a result of personal growth and development, rather than external factors alone.

**Imperfect Action:** Imperfect action refers to the concept of taking action without waiting for all the details to be perfect or the conditions to be ideal. It means taking action even if it is not flawless or polished, and understanding that mistakes and failures are a natural part of the learning process. Imperfect action is often encouraged as a way to overcome procrastination and fear of failure, and to gain momentum towards achieving goals.

**CFO (Chief Fun Officer):** The CFO, or Chief Fun Officer, is a term used to describe the man in a relationship taking the lead in creating an enjoyable and fun atmosphere in the home. This means taking responsibility for planning and organizing activities that both partners can enjoy together, such as date nights, weekend getaways, or even just spending quality time together at home.

Being a CFO can help to inject more excitement and energy into the relationship, which can have a positive impact on the overall health of the relationship. It also shows a willingness to prioritize the happiness and well-being of the couple and helps to build a sense of trust and connection between partners.

In addition to planning and organizing activities, being a CFO also involves being creative and spontaneous in the moment, such as initiating a game or activity, or simply making a joke to lighten the mood. It's about finding ways to make each other laugh, relax, and enjoy each other's company.

Ultimately, being a CFO means recognizing that fun and playfulness are important components of a healthy relationship and taking an active role in creating and maintaining that sense of joy and connection.

**Boundaries:** the limits or guidelines that an individual sets for themselves and their partner in order to maintain their physical, emotional, and psychological well-being while also promoting mutual respect and trust in the relationship.

For example, a married man may set boundaries around how he expects his wife to communicate with him during arguments. He might communicate that he feels disrespected when his wife raises her voice or uses insulting language and request that she refrain from doing so in the future. By setting this boundary, the man is communicating his need for respectful and healthy communication in the relationship and is taking a proactive step towards preventing conflict and maintaining a positive dynamic with his partner.

It is important to note that setting boundaries is not about controlling or manipulating one's partner, but rather about establishing healthy guidelines for behavior that promote mutual respect, trust, and well-being in the relationship. Both partners should be open to discussing and negotiating boundaries in a respectful and compassionate manner, with the goal of building a stronger and more fulfilling relationship.

**Sex Frame:** a mindset or approach that prioritizes and acknowledges the importance of intimacy and sexuality within the relationship. It involves intentionally creating a sexual undertone in interactions with your spouse and communicating that you view them as a desirable and sexual partner. This can help to deepen the emotional and physical connection between partners and enhance the overall quality of the relationship.

# About the Author

Doug Holt is not just a businessman; he's a visionary, a mentor, and a guide in the complex landscape of modern entrepreneurship. With a portfolio of companies all designed to empower business owners to thrive both professionally and personally, Doug's influence reaches far beyond the boardroom.

At the heart of his mission lies The Powerful Man, a transformative initiative aimed at helping businessmen evolve into better husbands, fathers, and community leaders. It's not about sacrificing business or self; it's about harmonizing all aspects of life to create something truly epic.

But who is Doug Holt beyond the titles and accolades? He's a father and a husband, a trusted friend and advisor. He's an entrepreneur with an adventurer's spirit, an investor with a regular guy's touch. Whether it's unraveling the mysteries of business over a fine glass of wine or exploring new horizons with a cup of coffee in hand, Doug's approach is as refreshing as it is insightful.

His clients see him not just as a professional guide but as a friend, someone who understands the intricacies of business and life. Doug's true passion? Helping business owners break free from stagnation, gain crystal-clear clarity, and seize control of their dreams. It's not just about business; it's about living the life you've always envisioned.

Join Doug on this journey and discover the path to a life that's not just successful but profoundly fulfilling.

Made in the USA
Middletown, DE
02 September 2024